The West Yorkshire Playhouse

Johnson Over Jordan

By J B Priestley

Director **Jude Kelly**
Designer **Rae Smith**
Composer **Sarah Collins**
Lighting Designer **Chris Davey**
Sound & Video Designer **Mic Pool**
Movement Advisor **Liz Rankin**

First performance of this production
Quarry Theatre
West Yorkshire Playhouse
29 August 2001

West Yorkshire Playhouse
Quarry Hill
Leeds LS2 7UP
www.wyp.co.uk
Tickets and information 0113 213 7700

Yorkshire Arts

THE COMPANY

Nicholas Blane George Noble/Millionaire/Madame Vulture/Don Quixote
Ken Bradshaw Doctor/Charlie/Barman
Clare Burt Nurse/Schoolmistress/Lottie Spragg/Doctor
Avril Clark Jill Johnson/2nd Examiner
Charlie Hayes Freda Johnson/Newspaper Seller/A
Jeanne Hepple Mrs Gregg/1st Examiner/Big Harry the Snout/
Mrs Morrison
Bernard Lloyd Mr Clayton/2nd Millionaire/Compere/Albert Goop
Simon Quarterman Richard Johnson/Newspaper Seller/B
Daniel Stewart The Figure
Patrick Stewart Robert Johnson

Emma Garner and **Sarah Collins** Musical Performers

All other parts played by members of the company

Dramaturg **Paul Taylor**
Assistant Director **Joss Bennathan**
D.S.M. **Porl Cooper**

Produced in association with Duncan C Weldon
for Triumph Entertainment Ltd.

BSL interpreted performances: Tuesday 11 September, 7.30pm
BSL interpreter: **Alan Haythornthwaite**
Audio-described performances: Thursday 13 September, 2pm and
Tuesday 18 September, 7.30pm
Audio-describers: **Anne Muers** and **Doreen Newlyn**

THERE WILL BE NO INTERVAL FOR THIS PRODUCTION

Smoking in the auditorium is not permitted. Please ensure that
mobile phones, pagers and digital alarm watches are SWITCHED
OFF before you enter the auditorium.

THE COMPANY

NICHOLAS BLANE
George Noble/Millionaire/Madame Vulture/Don Quixote

Theatre credits include: **How the Other Half Loves** (Bristol Old Vic); **A View from the Bridge** (Bolton Octagon); **I Have Been Here Before** (Worcester Swan Theatre); **The Duchess of Malfi, A Midsummer Night's Dream** and **Pravda** (Lancaster); **When the Wind Blows** and **Ubu** (Harrogate); **The Norman Conquests** (Nottingham Playhouse); **The School for Scandal** (Birmingham Repertory Theatre); **'Tis Pity She's a Whore** (Dundee); **Single Spies** (Farnham); **Doctor Faustus** (Young Vic); **Cyrano de Bergerac** and **The Taming of the Shrew** (RSC); **42nd Street** (Theatre Royal Drury Lane); **Fuente Ovejuna, Ghetto, Richard III** and **King Lear** (Royal National Theatre). Television credits include: **Trial and Retribution, Dalziel and Pascoe, Great Expectations, The Piglet Files, Heartbeat, Emmerdale, Reckless, Cracker** and **Coronation Street**.

KEN BRADSHAW
Doctor/Charlie/Barman

Theatre credits include: **Half A Sixpence, Spring and Port Wine, Macbeth, Enjoy, Intimate Exchanges** and **The Cucumber Man** (West Yorkshire Playhouse); **Blue Remembered Hills, A Naughty Night To Swim In** and **Bedevilled** (Sheffield Crucible); **Wizard Of Oz, The Mikado, Derby Day, Dancing at Lughnasa** and **Talent** (Bolton Octagon); **Venice Preserv'd** (Royal Exchange); **Stags & Hens** (Oldham Coliseum); **Doctor Faustus** and **The Caucasian Chalk Circle** (Liverpool Everyman); and **King Lear** (Kaboodle Productions). Television credits include: **Casualty, Julius Caesar, Time Treasures, Police 2020, Reckless, Coronation Street, Children's Ward, And The Beat Goes On, Heartbeat, This Is Personal, Blind Ambition, Where the Heart Is** and **Shipman**.

CLARE BURT
Nurse/Schoolmistress/Lottie Spragg/Doctor

Theatre credits include: **Broken Glass** (West Yorkshire Playhouse); **Moving Susan** (Greenwich Theatre); **Pal Joey** (Chichester Festival Theatre); **Into the Woods, Nine** and **Company** (Donmar Warehouse); **Harlequinade/Separate Tables** (King's Head); **Cat on a Hot Tin Roof** (Dundee Rep); **Moll Flanders** (Lyric Hammersmith); **The Hired Man** (Haymarket/Astoria London); **Sunday in the Park with George** (Royal National Theatre). Television credits include: **Company, The Audition, Wednesday at Eight, The Bill, A Woman of Substance, Blood and Lymeswold, Try Me, Enchanted Evening, Solace, ...And On, And On..., Spectator, Thoughts and Change** and **Breakpoint**. Film credits include: **Intimacy, The Dance of Shiva** and **Scream for Help**. Radio credits include: **Cabaret, Company** and **In With the Old**.

AVRIL CLARK
Jill Johnson/2nd Examiner

Theatre credits include: **A Slight Witch** (Birmingham Rep); **The Comedy of Errors** and **Augustine's Oak** (Globe Theatre); **The Comic Mysteries** (Oxford); **The Duchess of Malfi** (Cheek By Jowl international tour); **The Hypochondriac** (Cambridge); **Eurovision** (Drill Hall); **The Maple Tree Game** (West Yorkshire Playhouse); **Hamlet** (Chester Gateway); **Richard II, The Fool, The Love Girl and the Innocent** and **Thirteenth Night** (RSC); **Early Morning, Camille** and **Happy End** (Glasgow Citizens'); **Top Girls, The Ruling Class, On the Razzle** and **A Flea in Her Ear** (Leeds Playhouse). Television credits include: **The Bill, Maria's Child, Hetty Wainthropp Investigates, Pie in the Sky, A Wanted Man, Jane Eyre, London's Burning, House of Elliott, Rumpole** and **Eleni**.

CHARLIE HAYES
Freda Johnson/Newspaper Seller/A

Theatre credits include; **House and Garden** (Royal National Theatre); **House and Garden, A Listening Heaven, Dot Com, Hobson's Choice, Callisto 7, Doll's House** and **The Boy Who Fell into a Book** (Stephen Joseph Theatre Scarborough); **The Last Girl** (Riverside Studios, New Play Festival); **The Suitcase Kid** (Brix Theatre and BAC); and **Peter Pan** (Eye Theatre, Suffolk); **Tatiana in Colour** (Southwark Playhouse). Television credits include: **Doctors, Holby City, The Bill, Wycliffe, Fifteen Storeys High** and **Island**. Film credits include: **Harrow Alley** and **Washing Day**.

JEANNE HEPPLE
Mrs Gregg/1st Examiner/Big Harry the Snout/Mrs Morrison

Jeanne last appeared in Leeds playing opposite Laurence Olivier in Ibsen's **The Master Builder** for the Royal National Theatre. Other credits for the RNT include: **Uncle Vanya, St Joan** and **The Crucible**. Seasons at the RSC include: **The Devils, Becket, Women Beware Women** and **As You Like It**. After moving to America, Jeanne's Broadway stage credits included **Inadmissable Evidence** and **How The Other Half Loves**. She also expanded her interests into producing, teaching and directing. Jeanne appeared earlier this year in **The Daughter in Law** (Orange Tree Theatre). Television credits include **The Doctors** and **Midsomer Murders**.

BERNARD LLOYD
Mr Clayton/2nd Millionaire/Compere/Albert Goop

Bernard's many theatre credits include: **The Threepenny Opera** (Contact Theatre, Manchester); **Three Sisters** (Sheffield Crucible); **Still Time** (Royal Exchange, Manchester); **Fiddler on the Roof** (West Yorkshire Playhouse); **The Fawn** and **Le Cid** (Royal National Theatre). He has appeared in many productions for the RSC including: **Twelfth Night, The Winter's Tale, Troilus and Cressida, Henry V, A Doll's House** and **Henry IV Parts 1 & 2**. Television credits include: **Coronation Street, McCallum, Casualty, Inspector Morse, Under Milk Wood, Poirot** *and* **A Christmas Carol**.

SIMON QUARTERMAN
Richard Johnson/Newspaper Seller/B

Simon trained at the Central School of Speech and Drama and the National Youth Theatre. Theatre credits include: **The Young Idea** (Chester Gateway). Television credits include: **Swallow, Murder Rooms, Victoria and Albert, Lorna Doone, Family Tree, Down to Earth, The Sleeper, Midsomer Murders** and **Holby City**.

DANIEL STEWART
The Figure

UK theatre credits include: Krause in the world premiere of Tennessee Williams' **Not About Nightingales** (Royal National Theatre); **Left** (Royal National Theatre Studio); **The Country Wife** (Greenwich Theatre); **House of Mirth** (Cambridge Theatre Co.); **Macbeth** (Waterside Studio Theatre). In the United States: **Not About Nightingales** (Broadway run); **Jimmy Carter was a Democrat** (Clubbed Thumb); **Closer** (Portland Centre Stage); **The Beauty Queen of Leenane** (Syracuse Stage); **The Importance of Being Earnest, Othello, The Foreigner** and **Oklahoma!** (Hillside Rep., Los Angeles); **A Midsummer Night's Dream, Our Town, Amadeus** and **The Winter's Tale** (SSC). Television and film credits include: **Space: Above and Beyond**, **Death Train** and **Star Trek: The Next Generation**.

PATRICK STEWART
Robert Johnson

Theatre credits include: **Who's Afraid of Virginia Woolf**, for which he won the Fringe Best Actor Award (Guthrie Theatre and Young Vic); **Ride Down Mount Morgan** (Broadway); **A Christmas Carol,** for which he won a Best Actor Olivier Nomination, a Best Entertainment Olivier Award ands a Drama Desk Award (Broadway and the Old Vic); **Othello** (Shakespeare Theatre, Washington DC); **The Tempest** (NY Shakespeare Festival and Broadway); and **Yonadab** (Royal National Theatre). Credits for the RSC include: **The Winter's Tale, Titus Andronicus, The White Guard, Hippolytus, Antony and Cleopatra** (Best Supporting Actor Olivier Award), **The Merchant of Venice** (Best Actor Olivier Nomination), **The Bundle, Every Good Boy Deserves Favour, That Good Between Us, Bingo, The Iceman Cometh, Hedda Gabler, Uncle Vanya, Coriolanus, Julius Caesar, Enemies, Occupations, The Balcony, A Midsummer Night's Dream, Richard III, The Two Gentlemen of Verona, The Tempest, King John, Bartholemew Fayre, The Silver Tassie, Troilus and Cressida, Much Ado About Nothing, As You Like It, King Lear, The Investigation, The Revenger's Tragedy, Hamlet, Henry V, Henry IV Part I** and **II.** Television credits include: **A Christmas Carol, Moby Dick, Canterville Ghost, Star Trek: The Next Generation, The Mozart Inquest, Maybury, Smiley's People, The Anatomist, Hamlet, Tinker, Tailor, Soldier, Spy, Miss Julie, Oedipus Rex, I, Claudius, North and South, Joby, Antony and Cleopatra, The LoveGirl and the Innocent, The Artist's Story** and **Fall of Eagles**. Film credits include: **X-Men, Star Trek: Insurrection** and **First Contact, Conspiracy Theory, Masterminds, Dad Savage, Safe House, Jeffrey, Robin Hood: Men in Tights, L.A. Story, Lady Jane, Lifeforce, Dune, Excalibur** and **Hedda**.

CREATIVES

JOSS BENNATHAN
Assistant Director

Trained at: Goldsmiths' College London; Temple University, Philadelphia; RADA/Kings' College, London. Theatre directing includes: **Landscape of the Body** (Southwark Playhouse); **Our Town Story** (Millennium Dome); **The Revenger's Tragedy** and **The Country Wife** (Present Moment at The Bridewell); **Much Ado About Nothing** (London Centre for Theatre Studies); **Soft Times Remix, Relics** and **Big Bang** (ARC Theatre Ensemble); **Mrs Freud And Mrs Jung** (Pentameters/Buxton Festival). Devised work, here and in the USA, includes: **We All Come From Somewhere Else, Arrival, Wild Justice, The Sin Eater, Heart's Desire** and **Inc**. Joss is also author of **Developing Drama Skills 11-14, Performance Power** and scenes for **Late** (Radio 4).

SARAH COLLINS
Composer & Musical Performer

Sarah studied music at The City University and composition at Sussex University (with Jonathan Harvey). Ensembles written range from 2 cellos, through to 5 tubas and trombone with drum kit, 7 strings with 5 male voices and electric guitar, to the European Union Baroque Orchestra. Sarah has a wide experience in theatre and dance; and extensive composing and performing work in these fields. Rae Smith and Sarah Collins have been working on a large-scale opera piece **Terminatrix** supported by The English National Opera Studio, and the Royal National Theatre Studio. She is currently writing a string quintet based on her daughter's E.E.G. pattern. She is also continuing her one-minute opera series based on living film stars.

CHRIS DAVEY
Lighting Designer

For the West Yorkshire Playhouse Chris has lit: **Broken Glass, The Comedy of Errors, Half A Sixpence, The Colour of Justice** and **Love**. Recent designs include: **My One and Only** (Chichester Festival Theatre)**; Jekyll and Hyde** (Northern Ballet Theatre); **Guys and Dolls** (Sheffield Crucible Theatre); **The Force of Change** (Royal Court); **Out in the Open** (Hampstead Theatre); **The Car Man**, Winner of Best Musical Event, Evening Standard Awards (Adventures in Motion Pictures, tour and Old Vic); **Honk!** (National tour); **Closer**, winner of Best Lighting Design by the Irish Times (Abbey Theatre, Dublin); **Baby Doll** (Albery Theatre, Royal National Theatre and Birmingham Rep). He has worked extensively at the Royal Exchange, Manchester and Grange Park Opera. Designs for the Royal Shakespeare Company include: **Romeo and Juliet, A Midsummer Night's Dream, Everyman** (also in New York), **A Month in the Country, Troilus and Cressida, The Comedy of Errors** (world tour), and **Easter**. Designs for Shared Experience Theatre company: **Mill on the Floss, Jane Eyre, Anna Karenina** and **War and Peace** at the RNT.

EMMA GARNER
Musical Performer

Born in Salford in 1976, Emma studied piano at RNCM, and Leeds College of Music with Julian Cima. After completing the Graduate Diploma in Music she did two further years of Postgraduate study in Contemporary Music. During this time she actively taught and performed in the Leeds area with *Charanga del Norte*, a ten-piece Cuban dance band. Emma has spent many years as a Musical Director for amateur theatre companies and has spent the last two years playing in theatre orchestras on cruise ships. She is now living and working in Leeds as a performer and teacher.

JUDE KELLY
Director

Jude Kelly is Artistic Director of the West Yorkshire Playhouse. Over the last ten years Jude has established the theatre as a centre of excellence on a local, national and international scale, developing a centre for the arts with a policy of access for all. Jude's stage credits include: **Beatification of Area Boy** (Europe, New York and Australia); **When We Are Married** with Dawn French (Chichester Festival Theatre and in the West End); **Othello** with Patrick Stewart (Shakespeare Theatre in Washington DC); and **The Elixir of Love** (ENO). Notable productions for the West Yorkshire Playhouse include: **The Seagull** and **The Tempest** with Sir Ian McKellen; **Deadmeat**, a digital opera; **Macbeth**; **Singin' In The Rain**, which was nominated for 4 Olivier Awards and won the Most Outstanding Musical Production Award (also at the Royal National Theatre). Recent television credits include: **How Wide Is Your Sky?** (Real Life Productions for Channel 4). In 1997 Jude was awarded the OBE for her services to the theatre. In 1998 she was appointed Vice-Chair of the National Advisory Committee for Creative and Cultural Education. Jude also represents Britain for UNESCO on cultural matters. In 1998 Jude was appointed to the RSA Council and in December 1999 Jude was appointed as a member of the Independent Television Commission.

MIC POOL
Sound and Video Designer

In a twenty-four year career in theatre sound Mic has been resident at the Lyric Theatre Hammersmith, the Royal Court Theatre, Tyne Theatre Company and toured internationally with Ballet Rambert. He has designed the sound for over 200 productions including more than 100 for the West Yorkshire Playhouse where he is currently Director of Creative Technology. He received a TMA award in 1992 for Best Designer (Sound) for **Life Is A Dream** and was nominated for both the Lucille Lortel and the Drama Desk Award for outstanding sound design 2001 for the New York production of **The Unexpected Man**. Recent theatre includes: **Art** (West End, Broadway and worldwide); **Shockheaded Peter** (Cultural Industry world tour and West End); **The Unexpected Man** (West End and Broadway); **Another Country** (Arts Theatre); **Hijra** (Bush Theatre/Plymouth Theatre Royal); **A Midsummer Night's**

Dream, The Seagull, Victoria, Romeo and Juliet and Twelfth Night (RSC); The Seagull, The Tempest, Smoking with Lulu, Blithe Spirit, Naked Justice, Broken Glass and Inconceivable (West Yorkshire Playhouse). Video work for theatre includes: Singin' in the Rain (West Yorkshire Playhouse and Royal National Theatre); The Turk In Italy and Il Trovatore (ENO); and Das Rheingold (New National Theatre Tokyo). Television includes the sound design for How Wide Is Your Sky? (Channel Four).

LIZ RANKIN
Movement Advisor

Liz is a Movement Advisor and is Winner of the Time Out Award for Bringing Theatre Alive with Movement. Theatre credits include: The Changeling, Phoenician Woman, Midsummer Night's Dream, Romeo and Juliet, As You Like It, Henry VI parts 1, 2 and 3 and Richard III (RSC); Shakespeare's Sonnets, Anna Karenina, Mill on the Floss, The Tempest, Mother Courage, War and Peace, House of Bernarda Alba and Jane Eyre (Shared Experience); Fireface (Royal Court); Arabian Nights (Young Vic); The Comic Mysteries and My Mother Said (Oxford Stage Co.); and Hunting Scenes from Lower Bavaria (The Gate). Credits as director, choreographer and performer include: Summat A Do Wi Weddins, which won the Place Portfolio Choreographic Award; Ooh Out Of Order, with and without performers with a disability; and Funk Off Green, which won the Capital Award, Scotland. She has also performed: for *DV8, Gloria Music Theatre*, and the *Grass Market* project (working with strippers); with CAT A Theatre Co performing in prisons and theatres; in Derek Jarman's Pet Shop Boys tour film; and in Connie Giannaris' Silences and Caught Looking. She choreographed Nancy Meckler's film Alive and Kicking and performed in Wendy Houston's films Dance for Camera and Touched.

RAE SMITH
Designer

Rae has previously designed Death of a Salesman at the West Yorkshire Playhouse. Design credits include: Henry VI part 3 (RSC); Street of Crocodiles and The Visit (Royal National Theatre); The Weir and Dublin Carol (Royal Court and Broadway); Juno and the Paycock and Endgame (Donmar Warehouse and New York). Current work includes: The Servant (Lyric); Magic Flute (Garsington Opera); Antartica (West End); and The Prince of Homburg (RSC). Rae has also directed and designed: Lucky (David Glass Ensemble); Mysteria (RSC); TX3 (ENO Studio); and is currently performing live drawings in Frankenstein (RNT Studio). Portfolio - www.rae-smith.co.uk

PAUL TAYLOR
Dramaturg

Paul spent eight years lecturing in English literature at Oxford University before moving into journalism. He is currently Chief Theatre Critic and arts feature writer for *The Independent*.

AN ADVENTURE IN THEATRE

Johnson Over Jordan opens a season at the West Yorkshire Playhouse celebrating the work of JB Priestley. Four weeks prior to the play's opening **Paul Taylor** caught up with **Jude Kelly** and **Patrick Stewart** to discuss Priestley and to find out what attracted them both to a play that hasn't been performed for over fifty years.

PT   So Jude, why did you choose to reassess Priestley now?

JK   When I came to Yorkshire and the West Yorkshire Playhouse was being developed, we decided to name two of the rooms after two Yorkshire writers, Congreve and Priestley, but I have to say that I didn't have any sense of just what an extraordinary wealth of work he'd achieved. Reading *Johnson Over Jordan* I was struck by how ahead of its time and how risky it was. It made me ask myself who this man was, who would produce such a play at the height of his career. That's what made me read the rest of his work and realise that he should be reassessed.

I hadn't realised what a committed socialist he was and I didn't realise that he had been one of the most experimental writers of his generation with such a commitment to art for the person in the street. He didn't want to leave his fellows behind, but actually stay with them, keep with them and yet expand all the possibilities of what the human experience could mean for people.

I felt ashamed when I realised how little I knew about him and the extent to which I'd picked up a prejudice that he was a boulevard dramatist who'd created some middle of the road hits. And although obviously *An Inspector Calls* illustrates through Stephen Daldry's production how radical he was, I don't think people realise that this was Priestley's own intention, and was written into all his work. I thought that I couldn't be the only person who didn't know how comprehensive a literary figure he was.

PT   Patrick, have you had a long-standing interest in Priestley?

PS   I've had a historic connection with him in different ways: we're both Yorkshiremen, born in the West Riding a few miles apart; we're both socialists and both of us were brought up with trade union influence. I even lived for two years in the same Warwickshire village that he finally settled in later in his life and saw him often walking around the village taking exercise, but I was too shy and too intimidated by his dark appearance ever to approach him.

Another connection is that *An Inspector Calls* was the first radio drama that I ever participated in – it was a radio production of a stage version that we had done at the Sheffield Playhouse. I played the fiancé Gerald, but the mesh is more tightly woven because we recorded that production here at BBC Radio Leeds in 1962.

PT   You must also have seen him at Stratford, as he was on the board of the Royal Shakespeare Company?

PS   Yes he was and I'm angry with myself for not having found some way of approaching him.

Jude and I talked for a long time about doing a piece of work together and we both knew that we wanted it to be at the Playhouse. We talked about Shakespeare, we talked about Chekhov, we talked about the classics, and about commissioning a new work. But when Jude mentioned Priestley, I can't explain it, but it immediately turned a light on for me.

Johnson Over Jordan was a play that I had heard of, but knew mostly from a photograph of Ralph Richardson in an old theatre book, standing in profile against an old cyclorama with a black hat on. I had this instantaneous image from the play but when I read it I was astonished to find a JB Priestley that I had never encountered before.

PT   Did it deter you that it was his most spectacular flop?

PS   *(Laughs.)* Well I didn't know that at the time. There was contentment in that ignorance and because I knew that Ralph Richardson had been in it I assumed that it had been a success. I only learnt that it had been considered a failure and had met a lot of critical opposition once we decided to do it. I had pigeonholed him as a playwright writing in a very conventional form, invariably in most of his popular plays, about domestic issues – the family is the centrepiece of play after play. And indeed there is a family in this play, but Priestley *explodes* that family, in the way that Stephen Daldry exploded the house in *An Inspector Calls*, and sends it out into a dream world - a limbo.

I was thrilled and excited by the experimental nature of the play; by the European expressionist influence; and that it seeks, in sometimes abstract ways, to examine questions of how a man has lived, what his values have been, and how he dies. It looked like a challenge and it was the prospect of the challenge that excited me.

PT   It's a huge role, but it seems to present a peculiar challenge because although Robert Johnson is the central figure, he doesn't drive the play forward in the way that mighty protagonists usually do? Is that so?

PS   I have just come from three pieces of work in which I have been playing the leading role; characters who have not only had the psychological complexities of the play as the luggage that they carry, but also had to provide the energy of it. That is a responsibility shared by all the other people in this play, but not much by Johnson, who is very much a reactive character. But it is in the nature of his reactions - the way in which he is sometimes a pushover and the times occasionally when he makes a stand about issues – that the role is especially interesting.

He is involved in a number of scenes of very fine writing, but may only have half a dozen lines in those scenes, so this in a sense too is going to present me with a different kind of challenge in the responsibilities of a leading role.

PT   And Jude, presumably a big technical challenge is the fact that *Johnson Over Jordan* is a play that deals entirely with an intermediate state – Johnson is dead at the start so there is nobody to verify or falsify what Priestley says. Does that make the production vulnerable to cynicism and ridicule?

JK   Yes, the problem with images of heaven or hell, or limbo or purgatory, or anything that is essentially unknown, is that it's like being handed a piece of paper and being told to write whatever you like, and only afterwards finding out whether or not people liked it. Frameworks are great things and touching on authenticity, or re-interpreting, is what we are used to dealing with. The interesting thing about this is that you are absolutely looking for theatre statements to represent feelings, which the whole audience are going to have to authenticate based on whether or not they find it emotionally credible.

Priestley was also very adventurous in that the play operates outside of any Christian metaphor – he deliberately pushes you outside of the ability to use biblical imagery. It is as frightening as being Johnson seems to have been frightening.

PT   You have to re-invent the play in some respects for 2001. Since 1939 there have been a huge number of technological advances; will the imagery of the play be different?

JK   Well one of the things that I found very important in *Johnson* was the whole story of memory, of how your memory is selective. You define yourself by what happens to you in your life, but actually what you choose to remember about your life is very selective. And every time something happens to you, you're more or less taking a mental film of it, cutting out all the bits when people are watching you and having their own thoughts about what is happening. Since the 1930s domestic photography, home movies and camcorders have all become increasingly part of the way that we capture what we think of as our existence. And I find that very exciting as a way of exploring it.

In terms of whether *Johnson* was a success or a failure, I wasn't entering into it in order to do a great revival, but I do feel that I want to pay homage to Priestley's risk-taking. It is a great responsibility, because although I don't think that Priestley considered it to be a masterpiece, he was incredibly proud to have done it and very sad that people didn't recognise him for having taken those risks. There is a responsibility in terms of saying I think that this play was worth writing and is still very much worth doing.

J B PRIESTLEY
Tom Priestley

The 1930s were a decade of intense activity for JB Priestley. He wrote at least five novels, three major works of non-fiction, fourteen full-length plays and more than 450 articles. One might have expected him to ease up after the considerable success of *The Good Companions* and *Angel Pavement*. He was after all a professional writer who depended entirely on his writing to support his family. More probably that success gave him the freedom to move into other fields, especially the theatre. He had been drawn to the theatre in all forms from his youth, and always felt it suited his writing talent better than fiction. He could write his plays quickly in a great burst of creative energy, after first thinking them through in his head. I can remember him pacing the hall on days when he had to travel during his normal writing hours, and I sensed that he was off in another dimension. Of course the 1930s went from the Slump to the start of the War against the Nazis, a period of intense political activity. My father could not distance himself from that, feeling the need to comment on events and to express intuitively the concerns of ordinary people, as well as satisfying his own creative impulse.

Johnson Over Jordan was the last play my father wrote before the start of the 1939 war. It was the most obviously experimental of all his plays, combining all the resources of theatre available at the time. He first tried it out at the Bradford Civic Playhouse (now the Priestley Centre for the Arts) and returned with a rewritten version 3 weeks later. It opened in London on 22 February 1939 at the New Theatre, and later transferred to the Saville Theatre, when he made further changes to the text. Ralph Richardson, a regular collaborator of Priestley's, played Johnson to critical acclaim, but the play itself had a mixed reception; while some found it unsatisfactory, others were moved intensely. JB wrote of it: '*Johnson Over Jordan* must not be regarded as a play about life-after-death: it is rather a biographical-morality play'. He dedicated it 'with thanks and good wishes to all who shared with me this adventure of the theatre'.

(*Tom Priestley has worked in films as Feature Film Editor and directed the documentary* Time and the Priestleys *with and about his father. Latterly he has lectured on editing, and is a Guest Tutor at the National Film and TV School. Now retired, he is currently Administrator of the JB Priestley Estate, Vice President of the JB Priestley Society and President of The Priestley Centre for the Arts in Bradford.*)

J B PRIESTLEY
Judith Cook

There had never been anything like it in Bradford, averred one of the local MPs in the aftermath of the street battles which took place in the city in the summer of 2001. They were frightening, worrying and their origins still, to some large extent, unclear. But the MP was wrong. Bradford, in earlier centuries, had indeed seen violence on the streets and some of the same triggers were present: poverty, hardship, deprivation and a feeling of powerlessness. Ethnicity, however, was not an issue in the first fifty years of the nineteenth century when the disaffected people took to the streets.

'For many people in Bradford,' wrote local historian Peter Holdsworth, 'the first fifty years of the 1800s must have been hell on earth. Dire poverty, sickness, infirmity, near starvation, drunkenness and the dread of horrific old age abounded in a town where working conditions were often appalling and where bare-footed children in rags, stinking cellar dwelling and cheap brothels were commonplace. No wonder there was perpetual unrest and outbursts like the 1826 riot at Horsfalls' steam power loom mill in the North Wing when unemployed hand combers and weavers rioted with the result that two were killed and many more wounded.'

As late as Jack Priestley's grandfather's day conditions were still so bad that a surveyor reported: 'Masses of filth in all directions giving off foul stenches.' Medical men issued cholera warnings. This is not irrelevant for this is the background which was to produce the man. His father, Jonathan, was born in 1861, the son of an illiterate but skilled craftsman in the woollen mills and a young woman who was possibly a daughter of one of the Scots' families which came south looking for work in the mills, mines and manufactories of the north of England.

Priestley's grandfather died young but he remembered his grandmother clearly and with affection. 'When I was very young we had my grandmother living with us, and whenever my parents went out for the evening, my grandmother fed and entertained me. After we had eaten our rice pudding, she revealed to me the daily life and customs and folklore of the West Riding in the 1840s and 1850s. Ten university lecturers and twenty certified teachers could not have given me as much as she did: in sheer quantity yes, but not in quality. What was there, illuminating everything, was the magic that begins with personal experience and demands a certain detachment, close to wonder.'

Priestley's father, Jonathan, was born in 1861 and did so well at school that by some 'miracle of thrift', as his son put it, money was found to send him to a teacher training college, a rare route for a working-class boy without money: the usual route into the profession was through years spent as an ill-paid, uncertified pupil teacher. The horrors endured by the poor in Bradford would influence Jonathan Priestley throughout his working life. While things had improved somewhat, he had grown up surrounded by poverty and seen the abuse of the underprivileged. Conditions for workers were still far from satisfactory. He was a cradle socialist, considering any other philosophy unthinkable though, having said that, he was never doctrinaire, an attitude he was to bequeath to his son.

Jonathan had witnessed with his own eyes the result of the terrible strike at Manningham Mills when police and strikers fought a pitched battle in Town Hall Square, resulting in a number of the latter being seriously injured. Eventually infantry with fixed bayonets had to be brought in to form a barrier across the main road and restore order. One of the results had been the emergence of the Independent Labour Party which Jonathan Priestley joined. When he became headmaster of Green Lane School later, he was one of the first headmasters in the country – if not *the* first – to provide free school dinners for poor pupils.

In 1891 he married Emma Holt and the couple set up home in 34 Mannheim Road, in a respectable area known locally as 'the German quarter'. There was a close trading connection between Bradford and Germany; some local businesses were German-owned and a number of German and German-Jewish families had settled in that area. Priestley's mother was a lively young woman (with a hearty laugh), who may have helped her brother in his famous pub in Green Lane, The Volunteer (known as 'Holt's' after its landlord). Emma died at the age of thirty-one when Priestley was only two years old, one of a number of family members who died of cancer, as did his first wife, Pat. All had lived downwind of the huge chimney which dominated the city, a chimney which released chemicals from dyes into the atmosphere.

Jonathan married again, a stepmother much loved by Priestley. Jonathan's two consuming passions were education and socialism – he was a born teacher – and he encouraged his son to work for a scholarship to grammar school. But when Priestley reached the age of sixteen, his father's hope of him going into further education, even University, were not to be realised. Priestley wanted to leave school. To his amazement his father, who never had a good word to say about the wool industry, told him he should go into the trade, albeit in an office, and give himself a good start in life. That way, he was told, he could acquire a nice girl, a house of his own, a piano and a pram... But to Jonathan and his friends, 'the wool man' would always be the enemy of teachers and the good life. A composite and symbolic 'wool man' was the image used to represent capitalism in socialist cartoons.

This background was, therefore, one of the strongest influences on Priestley the man. It made him questioning, a believer in social justice – and no one who has read the wonderful and moving *English Journey* can doubt that for a moment – outspoken and, when he felt it necessary a campaigner, though never a 'joiner' in the ordinary sense.

The second major influence in his early life was that of the 1914-1918 War which he endured from first, to almost last, in the trenches. It is difficult to unravel from his own writings why he volunteered so enthusiastically on the first possible day in August 1914 at the age of nineteen. Unlike Robert Graves and many other writers, he did not write about the War or his experiences in it, until forty years later, and it may well be that it is with a kind of wishful thinking that he says he did not rush off 'with a herd of half-plastered chums' to join the local battalion of the West Yorkshire Regiment (later known as 'the Bradford Pals'). He quotes *Henry IV Part II* (his love of Shakespeare never left him), when the tailor, Feeble, is conscripted by Falstaff for the ongoing civil war: 'By my troth, I care not: a man can die but once. We owe God a death. I'll ne'er bear a base mind.' The young Jack Priestley had no such strong beliefs, but he once said that in September 1914 he had received a 'signal from the unknown'.

So he went off into the Inferno. A picture taken at the time looks like any one of the hundreds of thousands of young men who volunteered in the early days of the war, tens of thousands of whom were to die. He wrote extraordinary, and apparently uncensored, letters back from the front, the most horrifying of which enclosed some dried flowers about which he wrote: 'Enclosed are flowers, plucked from the parapet, probably growing out of dead men; there are plenty in these parapets. It's no uncommon sight to see a hand or a foot sticking out.'

He was wounded twice, the second time quite badly, but he was one of 'the lucky ones'. Two hundred 'volunteers' from the Bradford Pals were ordered 'over the top' on 29 June 1916 to check if heavy shelling had cleared the barbed wire. 'It hadn't and only forty men returned.' The remnants of other regiments were then hurriedly put together and, in the next action virtually none of them survived. In Yorkshire, crowds gathered daily outside the offices of the *Yorkshire Post*, *Sheffield Telegraph* and *Bradford Telegraph* waiting for the long lists of dead and wounded to be printed and posted up. The Western Front, wrote Priestley later, had 'become an abattoir in which thousands of young men were blown to pieces.'

He never recovered from his war experiences, In *Margin Released* he writes: 'I felt, as indeed I still feel today and must go on feeling until I die, the open wound never to be healed, of my generation's fate, the best sorted out and then slaughtered, not by hard necessity but mainly by huge, murderous, public folly.' Mrs Rosalie Batten, his last secretary, recalled that in his mid-eighties he would suddenly stop what he was doing and stare into space. 'Then he would say, "It was terrible, terrible…" and I knew he was thinking of the First World War.'

His friend and fellow-Bradfordian, John Braine, put it well: 'I think the real Jack Priestley died in August 1914 somewhere on the Western Front. He came out of it apparently without any neurosis but I think he actually did die. But a writer was born and what all those millions and millions of words were really written for was so that he wouldn't remember the 1914–1918 War.'

Of course this is all a world away from the popular image of Priestley, the immensely successful, extraordinarily prolific, writer who could switch easily between the disciplines of essayist, novelist and playwright. His remembered persona is that of the bluff Yorkshireman, puffing on a pipe, possibly imagined with a pint in his hand, giving his forthright views on the issues of the day – a straightforward, uncomplicated extrovert: Jolly Jack Priestley. Since his death he has also been cast in the unlikely role of a northern Don Juan flitting from woman to woman, which is unfair although he certainly did love women in general and some in particular, not least his third wife, Jacquetta Hawkes. His progress through life is seen as sure-footed, unshadowed, like a character out of his best-seller, *The Good Companions*. But the man underneath that public persona was given to deep introspection, insecurity and depression. A deep thinker, he was once described as 'the last of the Sages'. Least of all was he Jolly Jack Priestley.

He never, throughout his long life, was truly accepted by the metropolitan literary circles of his day. Not only did he not have the right background (even though he did achieve a degree at Cambridge), but he made free with his unsettling and unconventional ideas and did not pander to the latest fashionable taste. Nor did he suffer fools gladly. Worst of all, as a writer he was immensely successful. Not all that much has changed in such circles. But that is another story.

(*Judith Cook is an award-winning journalist, successful playwright and the author of eighteen books, including* Priestley *(Bloomsbury). She first met Jack Priestley in 1962, and subsequently visited him and Jacquetta Hawkes on a number of occasions. He encouraged her to begin writing books: 'It's time you were putting something between hard covers!'*)

JOHNSON OVER JORDAN
Paul Taylor

J B Priestley described his 1939 play *Johnson Over Jordan* as 'an adventure in theatre'. It turned out to be an adventure offstage as well as on. The piece was both his most searchingly experimental stage work and his most high-profile flop. As he later wrote, 'The fate of the play was as fantastic as its form'. It takes the most ordinary of men (a manager who began his career as a clerk) and places him in the most extraordinary of situations. Dying of pneumonia at fifty one, he re-engages with the life he apparently wasted in a jumbled posthumous dream of fears, secret longings, hopes and regrets, an experience which owes something to the Tibetan concept of the 'bardo', or prolonged intermediate state between physical death and ultimate release.

Because of the overblown Expressionist style of Basil Dean's original production, the critics concentrated predominantly – and negatively – on the outlandishness of Johnson's after-life journey which sends him first to the nightmare offices of the Universal Insurance Company (where his insecurities as family bread winner nervily surface), then to a sleazy fantastical nightclub (where he succumbs to the animal desires he had always suppressed) and finally to the Inn at the End of the World where he touchingly re-encounters those forgotten or unrecognised aspects of his existence that had warmed and illuminated it.

What was overlooked is the fact that the human and artistic importance of *Johnson Over Jordan* lies in the kind of figure it chooses to put through these experiences. The modernist writers of the period who derided Priestley as a middlebrow (Virginia Woolf notoriously described him as 'one of the tradesmen of letters') would also have dismissed Robert Johnson as a 'hollow man', one of those tepid souls who fail to qualify for either bliss or damnation because they lack the spiritual range. The fact, though, that Johnson is a fool, who has always been too anxious and inhibited to grab hold of his life, rather than a wicked man, is precisely what elicits Priestley's creative sympathies.

It is striking that, apart from the inclusion of the Christian burial service at the start, the play dispenses with any conventional religious framework. Deeply humanist, it does not present Johnson with a series of penitential tasks or with a purgatorial sentence. What is required of him is hauntingly passive: a recognition of all those inadequacies of communication and attentiveness that have left him hovering nervously on the threshhold of his life. Not that the 'bardo' state allows him to cross over that threshhold with any confident final flourish. The moments where human connections are at long last made are piercingly poignant because they are so fugitive and partial. The figures in his past never assemble for a group photograph of smiling forgiveness. There are no major chords. This is not like the analogous 1946 movie *It's A Wonderful Life* where the James Stewart character is redeemed from his sense of waste and unfulfilment by the eventual knowledge of how much good his self-sacrifice has achieved. Johnson's journey is less sentimental: its goal is to arrive at a point where he can see his life for what it has – and has not – been and then move on into the unknown.

This drama came at the end of Priestley's first playwriting decade, a decade characterised from the outset by an interest in experimenting with dramatic form. Showing how life can take frighteningly different routes depending on chance, unconsidered remarks and actions, his first play *Dangerous Corner* (1932) looks forward to more elaborate examinations of contingency and alternative realities, such as Alan Ayckbourn's multiple choice marathon *Intimate Exchanges* and the recent movie, *Sliding Doors*. By 1938, a theatre piece like *Music at Night* – in which Priestley attempts to dramatise the subjective responses of a group of people listening to the first performance of a violin sonata – was making Virginia Woolf's snobbery towards him look decidedly ironic, for it is the nearest equivalent in the drama of the period to her own explorations of the collective consciousness in novels like *The Waves. Johnson Over Jordan*, meanwhile, was the culmination of the sequence of Time-plays Priestley composed in the Thirties - *I Have Been Here Before,* with its Ouspensky-based idea of lives recurring along a spiral, and *Time and the Conways* in which the bleak second act jump into a shrunken future is softened by the conviction that the present is merely a two-dimensional cross-section of a larger four-dimensional reality where all our lived moments coexist.

In 1939, the critics and public were unanimous in their praise of the sublime final sequence where Ralph Richardson's Johnson – a small, forlorn figure, picked out against the immensity of the heavens – walked, with his bowler hat and briefcase, towards the stars. It was the style of what preceded this that was the bone of contention. Making a false equation between largeness of theme and scale of production, Priestley and his director, Basil Dean, had seized on the play as the chance to deploy to the limit all the resources of theatre and they were not slow to advertise their intentions in a publicity campaign that proved counterproductive. Hence the large cast, the twenty-strong orchestra, the two composers (one of whom was the young Benjamin Britten), the jagged irrelevant ballet of clerks and typists in Act One, the grotesque masks for the nightclub scene with their specially designed mobile mouths and the general sense of overkill. World-weary critics were able to recoil and claim that all of this was just 'our old friend Expressionism repeating its well-worn tricks'. James Agate, in his *Sunday Times* notice, resorted to lumbering parody of the insurance office scene: 'You know the kind of thing. A business magnate wants to write a letter, whereupon twelve typists appear joggling twelve imaginary typewriters while twelve office-boys lick twelve imaginary stamps'.

Though Priestley rejected the expressionist label, he did afterwards concede to Agate that 'if the play should ever be revived I should have it done in a simpler fashion'. In a letter written after the first night, his dramatist friend, James Bridie confessed that the emotional impact of the piece had left him unable to sleep, but he also complained that, in the excess of the staging, what got obscured was 'the grand simplicity and sincerity with which the play is conceived'. Now, in its first major revival since the 1940s, it is time for the virtues of *Johnson Over Jordan* to be rediscovered.

J(OHN) B(OYNTON) PRIESTLEY
(1894-1984)

A novelist, playwright, and essayist, JB Priestley's output was vast and varied - he wrote over 35 novels, over 35 plays and 40 works of non-fiction.

J B Priestley first gained international popularity with his novel *The Good Companions,* a tale about the adventures of a troupe of travelling players.

As a playwright, Priestley started in the 1930s with such popular plays as *Dangerous Corner* (1932); *Laburnum Grove* (1933); and *Time and the Conways* (1937), in which Priestley drew his ideas of Time from the works of J W Dunne and Ouspensky. Priestley also founded his own production company, English Plays Ltd, and from 1938-39 was director of the Mask Theatre in London.

Among Priestley's notable books were: *English Journey* (1934), a seminal work in arousing social conscience in the 1930s; *Literature and Western Man* (1960), a survey of Western literature over the past 500 years; and his memoirs, *Margin Released* (1962).

After the outbreak of World War II Priestley gained fame as 'the voice of the common people'. He was a patriotic radio broadcaster, second only to Churchill. At the early stage of the Cold War, he became known for his support for the Campaign for Nuclear Disarmament. From 1946-47 he was a UK delegate at UNESCO conferences.

As an essayist Priestley wrote for the 'middle brow' audience. The topics and themes are numerous. In his pamphlet *Letter to a Returning Serviceman* (1945), Priestley shared the common sentiment that Britain was obliged to rebuild along socialist lines after the war. In *Britain and the Nuclear Bombs* (1957) he argued for the moral superiority that unilateral nuclear disarmament would bring. *Disturbing (*1967) criticised contemporary playwrights for creating works that sought to 'disturb' a reading public already distressed by their own problems, and in *Particular Pleasures* (1975) he stated that works of art should meet some need, and not be evaluated on programmatic grounds.

Priestley married three times, in 1919 with Pat Tempest, who died young in 1925; then with Mary ('Jane') Wyndham Lewis, the former wife of the biographer and satirist D.B. Wyndham Lewis. In 1953 he married the archaeologist and writer Jacquetta Hawkes. They lived in Warwickshire in Kissing Tree House, situated near Stratford-upon-Avon. Together they co-wrote the travel book *Journey Down a Rainbow* (1955), which was based on their travels to Texas and New Mexico.

Priestley's prolific rate of production continued for nearly sixty years. From the age of 70 to 84 Priestley published another 21 books. Priestley refused both knighthood and peerage, but in 1977 accepted the prestigious Order of Merit. He died on August 14, 1984.

ARTS FOR ALL AT THE WEST YORKSHIRE PLAYHOUSE

Since opening in 1990, the West Yorkshire Playhouse has established a reputation both nationally and internationally as one of Britain's most exciting and active repertory theatres - winning awards for everything from its productions to its customer service. The Playhouse provides both a thriving focal point for the communities of West Yorkshire and theatre of the highest standard for audiences throughout the region and beyond. It produces up to 16 of its own shows each year in its two auditoria and stages over 1,000 performances, workshops, readings and community events, watched by over 250,000 people. The Playhouse regularly tours its productions around Britain and abroad.

Alongside its work on stage the Playhouse has an expansive and groundbreaking policy of education and community initiatives. As well as a busy foyer and restaurant which are home to a range of activities through the week, the Playhouse offers extensive and innovative education programmes for children and adults, a wide range of unique community projects and is engaged in the development of culturally diverse art and artists. It is this 'Arts for All' environment, as well as a high profile portfolio of international theatre, new writing for the stage and major productions with leading artists that has kept the Playhouse constantly in the headlines and at the forefront of the arts scene. Artistic Director Jude Kelly is a leading and visionary spokesperson for the arts, proving through the work of the Playhouse how theatres can play a critical role in society and the creative economy.

Leeds Theatre Trust Ltd.
Board of Governors

Chairman Councillor Bernard Atha
Board Members Barbara Barber, Alan Bottomley, Brian Bouttell, Mark Dickson, Councillor Peter Gruen, Councillor Janet Harper, Norman Hopwood, Oliver Jones, Jude Kelly, David Liddiment, John McInerney, Kay Mellor, Councillor Liz Minkin, Clare Morrow, Councillor Thomas Murray, Ken O'Connor, Diana Phillip, Arnold Reuben, Professor Philip Roberts, Tony Sharp, Councillor Neil Taggart, Councillor Christopher Townsley, Martin Wainwright

Staff

Jude Kelly Artistic Director (Chief Executive)
Maggie Saxon Managing Director (Company Secretary)
Ian Brown Associate Artistic Director
Paul Crewes Producer

Administration

Annette Ireland PA to the Artistic Director,
Dara Salsbury PA to the Managing Director

Arts Development Unit

Sam Perkins Head of Arts Development Unit
Lou Ford Community Projects Director*
Lisa Parrott Children's Officer
John Mee Partners Plus Co-ordinator*
Ruth Hannant Co-ordinator
Steve Burt, Jinny Lazenby, Kath Willis Advisory Teachers*

Schools Touring Company

Gail McIntyre Director
Amanda Strevett-Smith Workshop Development
Ysanne-Marie Morton Touring and Projects Co-ordinator

Associate Director

Mic Pool Creative Technology

Carpenters' Shop

Dickon Harold Master Carpenter
Philip Watson Deputy Master Carpenter
Andrew Dye and **Stephen Mainprize** Carpenters

Casting

Kay Magson Casting Director
Andrew Hall Special Projects Director

Catering and Bar

Sue Chappelow Catering and Commercial Manager
Sandra Gaffigan Deputy Catering Manager
Charles Smith Head Chef
Michael Montgomery Sous Chef
Simon Armitage and **Linda Monaghan** Commis Chefs
Louise Poulter Chef de Partie
Caron Hawley and **Esther Lewis** Kitchen Assistants
Andrew Cherry*, Gail Lambert, Carrie Edwards and **Kath Langton** Restaurant Assistants
Tara Dean-Tipple, Emma Ibbetson, Sarah Cremin, Victoria Dobson and **Victoria Burt** Catering Assistants*
Lornetto Mutteto, Qamar Zaman and **Kateeja Semdhoo** Coffee Shop Supervisors*
Malcolm Salsbury Bar Manager
Sally Thomas and **Hannah Thomas** Assistant Bar Managers
Anja Geissler, Emily Gray, Caroline Herbert, Oliver Limon, Anna Penney and **David Yates** Bar Assistants*

Company and Stage Management

Diane Asken Company Manager
Paul Veysey and **Karen Whitting** Stage Managers

Porl Cooper and **Nina Dilley** Deputy Stage Managers
Sarah Braybook and **Toby Heaps** Assistant Managers
Gemma Sharp Stage Management Placement

Corporate Affairs

Daniel Bates Director of Corporate Affairs
Kate Jeeves Development Manager
Rachel Coles Head of Press
Catherine Twite Press Officer
Sarah Jennings Corporate Affairs Assistant

Finance

Don Williams Finance Director
Teresa Garner Finance Manager
Coleen Anderson Finance Officer
Jenny Copley Cashier and Ledger Clerk
Susan Werbinski Salaries/Accounts Clerk

Marketing and Sales

Kate Sanderson Marketing Director
Nick Boaden Marketing Manager
John Polley Graphic Design and New Media Manager
Heather Bowen Graphic Design Officer
Kevin Jamieson Marketing Officer – Networks
Stephen Downie Marketing Officer – Programmes
Emma Lowery Marketing Assistant
Angela Robertson Sales Manager
Caroline Gornall Deputy Sales Manager
Lynn Hudson, Emma Lowery and **Mel Worman** Duty Supervisors
Carol Kempster Senior Box Office Assistant
Maureen Kirkby, Gaynor Flynn, Libby Noble, Sally Thomas, Joy Johnson, Pene Hayward, Philip Strafford and **Merryl Simpson** Box Office Assistants

Theatre Management

Helen Child Theatre Manager
James Barnett, Lee Harris and **Sheila Howarth** Duty Managers
Joy Johnson Assistant Duty Manager

Housekeeping

Doreen Hartley Domestic Services Manager*
Mary Ambrose, Eddy Dube, Harold Hartley, Betty Jenkinson, Michaela Singleton, John McHugh, Paul Robinson, Teresa Singleton, Sarah Wonnacott and **Amanda Brearley** Cleaners*

Security

Denis Bray and **Allan Mawson**

Customer Services

Kathy Dean, Jackie Gascoigne and **Leigh Exley**

Maintenance

Frank Monaghan Maintenance Manager
Roy Ellis and **Tony Wardle** Maintenance Assistants
Shane Montgomery General Services Assistant

Performance Staff

Andy Charlesworth and **Jon Murray** Firemen
Beth Allan, Rebecca Ashdown, Tanja Bage, Jo-Anne Brown, Mandeep Cheema, Sun-Young Chun, Li Daguerre, Maia Daguerre, Jon Dean, Shaun Exley, Simon Howarth, Clare Kerrigan, Jessica Kingsley, Sara Lovewell, Sally McKay, Jo Murray, Soazig Nicholson, Caroline Quinn, Alex Ramseyer, Louise Richards, Genevieve Say, Kateeja Sembhoo, Jamie Steer, Tom Stoker, Devi Thaker, Mala Thaker, Tal Varma, Naomi West and **Qamar Zaman** Attendants*
Beth Allan, Jackie Gascoigne, Clare Kerrigan, Jessica Kingsley Business Circle Co-ordinators*

Paint Shop

Virginia Whiteley Head Scenic Artist
Donna Maria Grummet Scenic Artist

Production Electricians

Stephen Sinclair Chief Electrician
Julie Rebbeck Deputy Chief Electrician
Neil Reynolds, Christopher Sutherland, Drew Wallis and **Adrian Whitworth** Electricians

Production Management

Mike Brown Technical Director
Suzi Cubbage Production Manager
Christine Alcock, Production Administrator

Props Department

Chris Cully Head of Props
Vic Carrera Freelance Prop Supervisor
Scott Thompson Supervisor
Susie Cockram and **Sarah Partridge** Prop Makers

Sound Department

Glen Massam Chief Sound Technician
Adrian Parker Deputy Sound Technician
Martin Pickersgill Sound Technician

Technical Stage Management

Martin Ross Technical Stage Manager
Michael Cassidy Senior Stage Technician
Julian Brown, Matt Heslop and **Nidge Solly** Stage Technicians

Wardrobe Department

Stephen Snell Head of Wardrobe
Victoria Marzetti Deputy Head of Wardrobe
Julie Ashworth Head Cutter
Selina Nightingale Cutter
Julia Walker Freelance Costume Prop Maker/Dyer
Sarah Marsh and **Nicole Martin** Wardrobe Assistants
Lucy Woodcock Freelance Wardrobe Assistant
Anne-Marie Snowden Costume Hire Manager
Kim Freeland Freelance Wig Supervisor
Vivian Brown Wardrobe Maintenance/ Head Dresser
Catherine Newton and **Joanne Daley** Dressers

*Denotes part-time

COMMUNITY PROJECT SPONSORS

New Opportunities Fund
The Heritage Lottery Fund

CHARITABLE TRUSTS

Audrey and Stanley Burton 1960 Trust
The D'Oyly Carte Charitable Trust
The Emmandjay Charitable Trust
Friends of the Playhouse
Harewood Charitable Settlement
Kenneth Hargreaves Charitable Trust
The Frances Muers Trust
L & D Cohen Trust
Lloyds TSB Foundation
Ragdoll Foundation
Clothworkers' Foundation

PRODUCTION THANKS

Hanco, Hall & Woodhouse Ltd., Richard Emmett at Engineering
Services Ltd., Highland Spring Ltd., Asda Stores Ltd., A&S Leisure
Group, The National Museum of Photography, Film and Television,
The Priestley Society, The Priestley Centre and The Priestley Library
at the University of Bradford.

West Yorkshire Playhouse
Corporate Sponsors

Sponsors of the Arts Development Unit
 PROVIDENT FINANCIAL

DIRECTORS' CLUB

Executive Level Members

 BTcellnet   CARLSBERG-TETLEY   Consignia   **Evans of Leeds**

Associate Level Members

TRUE TEMPER®   YORKSHIRE TELEVISION   Yorkshire Bank

Hammond Suddards Edge   **YORKSHIRE POST**

Director Level Members

Bacon & Woodrow	Le Meridien Queens
Bank of Scotland	Lloyds TSB
BWD Rensburg	NatWest
Convergent Communications	New Horizons
Crowne Plaza	Odgers Ray & Berndtson
GNER	Provident Financial
Godloves	Thompson Design
Kingston inbusiness	Yorkshire Dales Ice Cream
KPMG	

One Performance Sponsors

STS Ltd	**Inscape Investments**	**Leeds Massada Fellowship**
Half a Sixpence	The Comedy of Errors	Half a Sixpence

If you would like to learn how your organisation can become involved with the success of the West Yorkshire Playhouse please contact the Corporate Affairs Department on 0113 213 7274/5 or email corporateaffairs@wyp.org.uk

First published by William Heinemann Ltd

Published in 2001 by Oberon Books Ltd.
(incorporating Absolute Classics)
521 Caledonian Road, London N7 9RH
Tel: 020 7607 3637 / Fax: 020 7607 3629
e-mail: oberon.books@btinternet.com

A catalogue record for this book is available from the British
Library.

ISBN: 1 84002 248 5

Cover Design: Thompson Design
Cover Photograph: Quantum Photography

Printed in Great Britain by Antony Rowe Ltd, Reading.

Characters

AGNES
UNDERTAKER'S MAN
CLERGYMAN
MRS JOHNSON (JILL)
MRS GREGG
RICHARD JOHNSON
FREDA JOHNSON
MR CLAYTON
GEORGE NOBLE
JOHNSON
FOUR SECRETARIES
FIRST OLD MAN
SECOND OLD MAN
CLERK
EXAMINERS
SCHOOLMASTER
NEWSPAPER BOYS
POLICEMAN
THE FIGURE
BARMAN
SIR JAMES PORKER
HEADWAITER
STOUT WOMAN
CHARLIE
MADAME VULTURE
COMPERE-SCHOOLMASTER
GORILLA
YOUTH
PORTER
ALBERT GOOP
TOM
MORRISON
DON QUIXOTE
DOCTOR

Johnson Over Jordan was first produced at the New Theatre, London on 22 February 1939, with the following cast:

JOHNSON, Ralph Richardson

JILL, Edna Best

THE FIGURE, Richard Ainley

FREDA, Victoria Hopper

RICHARD, Christopher Quest

CLAYTON, Ernest Borrow

MADAME VULTURE, Emma Trechman

MRS GREGG, Violet Blyth Platt

STOUT WOMAN, Betty Shale

AGNES, Louise Frodsham

TOM, Grey Blake

Other parts played by:

George Hayes, Meadows White, Henry Hallatt, Stafford Hilliard, Wilfred Babbage, Lawrence Baskcomb, Tarver Penna, Albert Chevalier, Jack Lambert, Larry Silverstone, Michael Rose, Pamela Blake

ACT ONE

*After some music, which begins fiercely and frighteningly and then
sinks into a funereal melancholy, we find ourselves looking at the
hall of ROBERT JOHNSON's house, somewhere in one of the
pleasanter outer suburbs. There is not much to be seen: a door in the
centre that probably leads into the drawing-room, and on one side of
it a small table and a chair or two, and on the other side one of those
tall stands for hats and overcoats and sticks. What impresses us is the
atmosphere in here. It is at once cold and shuttered. There is something
chill and uneasy about the very light. Something is wrong; this is no
ordinary morning; and then we realise what we are in for when
AGNES the maid, in black and rather red about the eyes, comes in
followed by two or three middle-aged persons all in black, whom she
shows into the drawing-room. Yes, they are mourners, and they are
about to attend a little funeral service in the house before the remains
of ROBERT JOHNSON are taken to the cemetery. We gather from
the murmur of voices that these mourners are among the last, not the
first, to arrive. When AGNES has shown these people in, she looks
hesitatingly at the tall stand where the hats and coats are, makes up
her mind what to do, then with rather furtive haste takes some things
from the stand. A middle-aged UNDERTAKER'S MAN, who spends
nearly every morning in this strange atmosphere, has now entered,
and, after giving a quick glance at his watch, is now observing
AGNES.*

UNDERTAKER'S MAN: Them things his?

AGNES: (*Sniffily, whispering.*) Yes. I'm taking 'em out. I'm
taking 'em out. I'm sure it'll upset Mrs Johnson seeing
'em here. I know it would me. 'Ats and sticks – and he's
gorn.

UNDERTAKER'S MAN: (*Who has to be a bit of a philosopher.*)
That's right. And them things lasts longer than we do,
see? Makes you think a bit, that does, eh? But don't be
too long putting 'em away. We ought to be starting soon.
(*AGNES goes one way with her little pile of hats and coats
and does not notice that a glove has fallen on the floor. The
UNDERTAKER'S MAN does not notice the glove because
now, after looking again at his watch, he has gone the other*

way, only to return the next moment with an elderly CLERGYMAN, all ready for the service.)

UNDERTAKER'S MAN: Along 'ere, sir. I think they're all in but the family – and the family's upstairs waiting to come down.

CLERGYMAN: (*Rather impatiently.*) Yes, yes. Well we ought to begin quite soon.

UNDERTAKER'S MAN: (*Who often has to soothe clergymen.*) Shan't be two minutes now, sir. In here, sir.

(After showing the CLERGYMAN where to go, he goes off where AGNES went. The family must have been waiting for him to tell them all is ready, for now they come on, slowly, miserably, in deepest black. There is MRS JOHNSON, whose name is JILL, who is looking so terribly distressed that we cannot tell anything about her except that she is a woman in her late forties. She is supported, physically as well as morally, by her mother, MRS GREGG, who must be well on into her sixties and has now attended many funerals. Closely behind them come the two children: RICHARD, a nice-looking lad in his early twenties, and FREDA, a handsome girl a year or two younger; and they are both making a desperate effort to carry it off well. Just as this little procession nears the door, JILL sees the glove that AGNES dropped, gives a little cry, and picks it up.)

MRS GREGG: Never mind that. It's nothing, dear.

JILL: (*Who knows better.*) It's his glove – all that's left of him.

(This is too much for her and she sobs convulsively. MRS GREGG and the children try to comfort her, while the UNDERTAKER'S MAN hovers behind them.)

MRS GREGG: (*Who had her doubts before.*) Perhaps you'd better not attend the service, after all, Jill.

JILL: (*Struggling to be calm.*) No, mother, I'll be all right. I'm sorry. It was seeing that glove – so suddenly, like that – on the floor – as if people had been walking over it.

RICHARD: Don't think about it, Mother – please. We just haven't to think, this morning, that's all.

JILL: (*Still struggling.*) I'll be sensible.

(The UNDERTAKER'S MAN has now crossed to open the door for them, and his manner suggests that though he has

every sympathy with MRS JOHNSON, he must point out that the morning's grim programme must be got through in reasonable time.)

UNDERTAKER'S MAN: They're all ready when you are, Mrs Johnson.

(So JILL makes a last effort and in she goes, with the family, while the UNDERTAKER'S MAN holds the door open, then almost closes it and goes tip-toeing away. After a moment's wait, we hear the CLERGYMAN beginning the service in there.)

CLERGYMAN: (*Off.*) I am the resurrection and the life, saith the Lord; he that believeth in me, though he were dead, yet shall live; and whosoever liveth and believeth in me shall never die…

(But before we have time to ask ourselves what these strange words really mean, two late mourners have entered the hall. The first is MR CLAYTON, a spruce, rotund, prosperous old gentleman, and the other is GEORGE NOBLE, a middle-aged, conventional sort of chap, both in formal mourning. MR CLAYTON goes to the door, listens a moment, then closes it carefully, and joins NOBLE, who has been waiting hesitantly. Now they stand close together and talk in that rather sideways manner, with a loudish whisper, which indicates they are embarrassed. But they are men of the world and will make the best of it.)

CLAYTON: They've begun the service in there. No good going in now, eh?

NOBLE: Rather not. Wait until it's over, eh?

CLAYTON: (*Nodding, then somewhat abruptly.*) Can't say I mind, myself. Don't take much stock in these services, y'know. Comforting to the women, of course. Meeting in Heaven – and all that, eh? But if you ask me – when you're dead that's the end of you.

NOBLE: (*Who hasn't given it much thought.*) I shouldn't be surprised.

CLAYTON: Like to pay last respects, though. Knew poor Johnson very well. Did you?

NOBLE: Yes. Cousin. Noble's my name.

CLAYTON: Ah yes. Mine's Clayton.

NOBLE: (*With increased respect now.*) I've heard poor Robert talk about you, Mr Clayton. Chairman of the Board at his firm, aren't you?

CLAYTON: (*Rather glad of a chat.*) Yes. Remember Johnson coming to us as a junior clerk, thirty years ago. Worked his way up steadily. We thought a lot of him. Great loss to the firm. So young too. Fifty?

NOBLE: Just about. Fifty-one, I fancy.

CLAYTON: No age at all. And went off – like that. Wasn't in bed a week. Pneumonia, of course.

NOBLE: You never can tell, can you? And I'd have called Robert a pretty careful sort of chap.

CLAYTON: So would I. Careful, steady fellow, who always understood his responsibilities. That's why we liked him. Not easy to replace, I'll tell you.

NOBLE: Bad luck all round. Happily married too. And nice boy and nice girl, still very young. All comfortable, nicely settled.

CLAYTON: (*Rather indignantly.*) And suddenly goes – like that. And I can give him twenty years. No sense in it. No sense in it at all.

(*They do not say any more because now the UNDERTAKER'S MAN comes in and listens at the door. This reminds them that a funeral service is going on in there, and they are obviously embarrassed as they watch the man go out again.*) (*Dropping his voice a little.*) Better wait outside, I think now, eh?

NOBLE: (*Relieved at the suggestion.*) Just what I was going to suggest. Shouldn't like to be caught just standing here. (*So out they go, slowly, with unnecessary caution, and now the door opens, not because the service is over but because RICHARD is there, opening it, ready to sneak away himself but also to give his sister FREDA, who is taking it very hard in there, a chance to slip out and recover. We do not see her, however, but only just catch this glimpse of RICHARD, for now the lights are beginning to fade and through the growing dusk comes the voice of the CLERGYMAN continuing the service.*)

CLERGYMAN: (*Off.*) For man walketh in a vain shadow, and disquieteth himself in vain. He heapeth up riches, and cannot tell who shall gather them…

(*Now it is completely dark and the music has begun again, but it does not continue long in that strain but changes into something quicker and fiercer. Obviously the real JOHNSON is not lying in that oak box which the UNDERTAKER'S MAN is now having conveyed to the waiting hearse. What is happening to the real JOHNSON? Just as we are wondering this, we see him. That is all we see – JOHNSON's face strongly illuminated against a background of darkness. He is talking away in an odd confused manner, like a man in a delirium.*)

JOHNSON: ...They can say what they like, but I've a high old temperature... Look at the way things bend and waver and then go floating about... That's not normal... And corridors...long corridors...far too many long corridors...I noticed some corridors when they brought me in – you can't have a big nursing-home without corridors – but not as many as all that – and not so long... And a pretty penny this'll cost us before I'm out again... Fifteen guineas a week for the room, at least... then the doctors...and extras – all sorts of nonsense – and charge you the earth for 'em... Minute you take to your bed, money's poured out like water... Lucky I've been careful... Whatever happens, Jill ought to be all right... Never missed paying a premium...good company...one of the biggest and best insurance companies in the world... They oughtn't to try any tricks with her... I'll see they don't... Better write to 'em myself...good stiff letter... No nonsense... Miss Francis... Miss Francis...want you to take a letter... (*He appears to imagine he is back in his own office, and so calls for his secretary. In the world he is in now, a world we ourselves visit in dreams, you do not call in vain for anybody or anything, though the results are apt to get out of control. That is what happens now. We see that four secretaries, blank-faced girls all wearing tortoise-shell glasses and dressed alike, have grouped themselves round JOHNSON so that he sees one whichever way he turns. They carry notebooks, and indeed the lights that show us their faces seem to come from these notebooks.*)
Ah, there you are, Miss Francis.

33

FIRST GIRL: Yes, Mr Johnson.

JOHNSON: (*Rather wearily.*) Want you to take a letter.

SECOND GIRL: Yes, Mr Johnson.

JOHNSON: (*Making an effort.*) An important letter...to the Universal Insurance Company...

THIRD GIRL: Yes, Mr Johnson.

JOHNSON: (*After slight pause, tired.*) 'Dear Sirs...'

FOURTH GIRL: Yes, Mr Johnson?

JOHNSON: (*Confusedly.*) No, no...doesn't matter...you needn't bother, Miss Francis ...cancel that letter.

ALL FOUR GIRLS: Yes, Mr Johnson.

(*And all four quietly disappear, while JOHNSON tries to collect himself.*)

JOHNSON: No, no...letter won't do...that was what Mr Clayton always said, and he was right... If you want to do business, go and do it yourself, face-to-face... Quite right... If I want my money, no use merely writing a letter... They get millions of letters... Only thing to do is to go for the money myself... My money, isn't it? All honestly earned – years of hard work... Just say to them 'Look here, I want my money... As one business man to another, 'what about my money?' ...Forms to fill in – red tape – only to be expected, big company like that – enormous business – tremendous organisation... May have a little difficulty...business man myself, so quite understand... But I must have my money...

(*As soon as he has said this, the music bursts into a fast, clattering, nattering, nervy strain, and we see that JOHNSON is now surrounded by a number of clerks and secretaries, male and female, who are all busy exchanging documents, making notes, and so on, making very quick movements in a stylised fashion. Moreover, they are lit from below, and it is not easy to see them properly and they throw big confusing shadows. The total effect is irritating and then exhausting, as if we had been given a whole modern business man's day within one minute. And now through the clatter comes a loud, harsh, impersonal voice from a loud-speaker, bellowing.*)

VOICE FROM LOUD-SPEAKER: The time is four twenty-five – four twenty-five. All forms KRT three-seven-nine to be returned to Room Eighty-two by four thirty-five. All forms KRT three-seven-nine to be returned to Room Eighty-two by four thirty-five. The time is now four twenty-six.

(*And now the ballet of clerks hurries off. JOHNSON tries to stop the last of them but is not successful. The whole scene is now illuminated by a hard white light, almost dazzling. It is quite a big and high room, with enormous silvery doors at each side, and in the middle, the only furniture it has, a tremendous silvery desk raised on a dais, with a very big swivel chair at each side and one at the back. In front is a kind of settee made of the same silvery material. It all looks very modern, efficient and opulent, and quite inhuman. Seated in the big chairs at each side of the desk are two old men, worried old men with white hair, tinted spectacles, morning coats, and the look of dyspeptic millionaires. They have forms and enormous ledger-like volumes in front of them, and they turn the pages of these volumes in a quick desperate sort of fashion. High above the desk is one of those clocks that have no works and no compassion for our frailties, and above the clock is hanging a horrible white cluster of loud-speakers.*

JOHNSON, whom we now see clearly as a pleasant fellow in a dark business suit, looks at all this in bewilderment, then cautiously approaches the first old man, who is too busy to notice his existence.)

JOHNSON: Pardon me, sir, but would you mind telling me –

FIRST OLD MAN: (*Looking up, testily.*) I'm very busy, you know, my dear sir, very busy indeed.

JOHNSON: (*Taken aback.*) Sorry! (*He goes round to the SECOND OLD MAN.*) I wonder, sir, if you'd mind –

SECOND OLD MAN: (*Looking up, annoyed.*) What is it then, what is it?

JOHNSON: (*Apologetically.*) Well, you see, I don't seem to remember how I got here –

(*FIRST OLD MAN looks up and makes a tut-tutting noise.*)
I was in bed – as a matter of fact I wasn't feeling very well – had quite a temperature – and then – well –

SECOND OLD MAN: (*Who has no time for this stuff.*) Then what?

JOHNSON: (*Who cannot help being vague about it.*) Well, that's all I remember. Must have slipped out somehow and come along here. Loss of memory, I suppose. Nuisance! Making a fool of myself! Don't even know what I want here.

FIRST OLD MAN: (*Who does not need even to look up for this.*) Of course you do. You want your money. Wouldn't be here if you didn't.

JOHNSON: My money?

FIRST OLD MAN: (*Now condescending to look up.*) Yes, of course. You want your money. I want *my* money.

SECOND OLD MAN: (*Who won't be left out.*) And I want *my* money.

FIRST OLD MAN: We all want our money, don't we? Come, come, don't be childish, my dear sir.

JOHNSON: (*Apologetically.*) Sorry! But you see – I can't remember. I was ill, y'know – really ill. I overheard the doctor –

FIRST OLD MAN: Don't bother me with doctors. Plenty here if you want one.

SECOND OLD MAN: Wonderful medical staff here. But they won't get you your money, will they?

FIRST OLD MAN: (*Willing to stop work for a chat about money.*) How much are you expecting?

JOHNSON: (*Who cannot help feeling that this is pretty good.*) Oh – well – several thousands, y'know.

FIRST OLD MAN: (*Contemptuously.*) Several thousands!

SECOND OLD MAN: (*Perhaps the worse of the two, sniggering.*) One thousand, two thousand, three thousand! (*The two ancient and desiccated monsters cackle together and point contemptuously at poor JOHNSON, who watches them spread themselves in their chairs now.*)

JOHNSON: I don't see anything particularly funny about it.

FIRST OLD MAN: I cleared two hundred and fifty thousand on Consolidated Copper.

SECOND OLD MAN: I made a cool three hundred and fifty thousand out of National Nickel.

FIRST OLD MAN: I netted four hundred and fifty thousand out of International Iron.

SECOND OLD MAN: I cashed in for five hundred and fifty thousand out of Standard Steel.

FIRST OLD MAN: (*To finish this off.*) I wrote to the directors here and told 'em that to save time I'd accept, in settlement of my claim, one million and seven hundred and fifty thousand.

SECOND OLD MAN: (*To go one better.*) 'Gentlemen,' I wrote, 'we are men of few words. I'll make no further demands on you if you give me your cheque for two millions.'

(*JOHNSON, who has been sitting on the settee in front of the desk, turning to listen to first one and then the other, is now only about half the size he was at the beginning of this duet. He rises and walks round to the back of the desk, regarding the two old men with bewildered awe.*)

JOHNSON: Well of course, I don't wonder you were amused. This is big business, altogether out of my depth. I've heard and read about these transactions, but I've never been mixed up in them. You see, the firm I've been with all the time is just an old-fashioned firm of East India merchants – a good sound business, of course – but –

FIRST OLD MAN: (*Who has been looking at his form, and now interrupts ruthlessly.*) What was the National Debt in 1907?

JOHNSON: (*Bewildered.*) I don't know. Why?

FIRST OLD MAN: (*Consulting his form.*) It says here – question thirty-four in sub-section K – deduct your personal expenditure for the first quarter of 1907 from the National Debt of that year – but see Note 645 D. (*He looks for this.*) Omit in calculation of Debt half-yearly interest due on Consols. But see note on repayment of Indian Loans. (*He searches wildly, then cries in despair.*) I'll never do it. They know I'll never do it. They want to keep my money.

(*JOHNSON, who is now sitting in the chair at the back of the desk, stares at him in amazement, while the worried old man turns pages over and plunges wildly into calculations. The second one now raises a despairing voice.*)

SECOND OLD MAN: Brazilian Railways! Brazilian Railways! Add all dividends to British investors in Brazilian Railways from 1895 onwards. (*Turning to form again.*) But omit all earnings of Anglo-Brazilian

Investment Corporation. (*Adds in despair to the other two.*) There won't be time again, you'll see. Then I'll have to start all over again, with another form – quite different.

FIRST OLD MAN: (*Miserably.*) They're determined to keep our money.

SECOND OLD MAN: (*Suddenly changing his tone.*) What are you going to do with your money when you do get it?

FIRST OLD MAN: (*Looking up, not uninterested.*) I'm going to – er – oh, there was something – but I've forgotten.

SECOND OLD MAN: (*Proudly.*) I have the second-best collection of eighteenth-century French snuff-boxes in the world. Museum pieces all of them.

FIRST OLD MAN: (*Testily.*) You told me. Let's get on, let's get on. No time to waste. (*And they plunge into work again.*)

VOICE FROM LOUD-SPEAKER: Only seventeen more minutes for forms GTO seventy-six to four hundred and nine. Only seventeen more minutes for forms GTO seventy-six to four hundred and nine.

FIRST OLD MAN: (*Wildly.*) Did they say from seventy-six to four hundred and nine?

JOHNSON: Yes.

FIRST OLD MAN: Mine's GTO three-twenty-five. That means I've only seventeen more minutes.

VOICE FROM LOUD-SPEAKER: (*With sharp hint of correction.*) Sixteen and a half minutes.
(*The old man works like fury.*)
Robert Johnson!

JOHNSON: (*Startled, jumping up.*) Yes?
(*He looks at the loud-speaker as if expecting a reply from it, but what happens is that a clerk, not one of the posturing youngsters we have seen already but a solid, middle-aged, authoritative fellow, marches in, moving straight towards the SECOND OLD MAN, who is also buried in his ledger and forms.*)
(*Noticing the CLERK.*) Oh – I say.

CLERK: (*Firmly.*) Just a minute, please. (*To the SECOND OLD MAN.*) Have you completed your form of application?

SECOND OLD MAN: (*Desperately.*) Nearly, nearly, shan't be a minute, shan't be a minute. I'm not as young as I was, remember. My eyes bother me. Yes, don't forget that.

(*He tries to retain the form, but the CLERK firmly takes it from him and looks at it with contempt.*)

CLERK: You'd better come with me.

(*The SECOND OLD MAN rises sadly.*)

VOICE FROM LOUD-SPEAKER: (*Severely.*) All reference books to be returned to the office library.

(*The SECOND OLD MAN takes up his ledger and follows the CLERK out. JOHNSON watches all this with growing dismay. The FIRST OLD MAN, who has been working very hard with his form and huge volume, is now suddenly triumphant.*)

FIRST OLD MAN: I've got it. At last I've got it.

(*But one of the young clerks, repeating the phrase about reference books going back to the library, hurries in to take the book from the FIRST OLD MAN, who flings down his form and pen and buries his head in his hands in complete despair.*)

JOHNSON: (*With concern.*) Look here, can I do anything for you?

FIRST OLD MAN: (*Looking up, cynically.*) What! And then claim a share in my money? Not likely! You don't catch me that way. Oh no!

JOHNSON: (*Indignantly.*) I didn't want to catch you. And I don't want your money.

FIRST OLD MAN: That's what *you* say. And then you wouldn't want a twenty-five per cent interest afterwards, would you? Oh no, not at all! My dear sir, I'm a business man, and I learned how to look after myself before you were born.

JOHNSON: (*Beginning to be sceptical.*) I wonder.

VOICE FROM LOUD-SPEAKER: Forms GTO three hundred to three hundred and fifty, whether completed or not, must be returned at once to Room Forty-nine.

FIRST OLD MAN: (*Desperately.*) I won't go. I won't go.

(*But now the CLERK enters, carrying a long form, and looks sternly at the old man.*)

CLERK: (*Firmly.*) Room Forty-nine.

FIRST OLD MAN: No. This is the hundred and seventeenth time.

CLERK: Room Forty-nine at once, please.

(*The FIRST OLD MAN goes out wearily and the CLERK is following him when he is stopped by JOHNSON, who is now losing his patience.*)

JOHNSON: Now – look here.

CLERK: (*Briskly, consulting form.*) Robert Johnson?

JOHNSON: Yes, that's my name.

CLERK: (*Checking details from the form.*) Aged fifty. Married and two children, son and daughter. Manager for Messrs. Bolt, Cross and Clayton, East India Merchants.

JOHNSON: Yes. But –

CLERK: (*Cutting in.*) Here's your form.

(*He hands over the form, then turns away, but this is not good enough for JOHNSON, who stops him, not far from one of the big office doors.*)

JOHNSON: (*With the remnant of his patience.*) Just a moment, please.

CLERK: (*Unpleasantly.*) We're busy here, you know, very busy. Listen!

(*He opens the nearest door, and we hear the clatter of a very large office – typewriters, adding machines, ringing of bells, etc. But now JOHNSON really loses his temper.*)

JOHNSON: (*Shouting angrily.*) I don't care how busy you are. I want to know something.

CLERK: (*Very civil now.*) Certainly, Mr Johnson. What is it?

JOHNSON: I want to know where I am. What is this place?

CLERK: Central offices of the Universal Assurance and Globe Loan and Finance Corporation. Where you get your money.

JOHNSON: (*Remembering.*) Ah – yes, of course. My money.

CLERK: (*Smiling.*) We all have to have money, haven't we? Can't do without that.

JOHNSON: (*Rather confusedly.*) No, of course not. But – the trouble is, you see – well, I must have lost my memory… I've been ill… I was in bed – yes, in a nursing home… doctors coming all the time…two nurses…everybody looking worried… I must have wandered out somehow…

CLERK: (*With the air of one dealing with a child.*) Quite so.
Well, all you have to do is to fill in your form properly
and then we give you your money. You can't get out of
here until you have your money, so of course you have
to stay here until you've filled in your form properly.

JOHNSON: (*Rather dubiously.*) Yes – well – that's reasonable
enough. Filled in plenty of forms in my time – all kinds
– (*Glances at the huge form in his hand.*) Pretty elaborate
sort of thing, though – isn't it? Complicated questions.
Is – er – all this necessary?

CLERK: Most certainly. You must concentrate, Mr Johnson,
concentrate.

JOHNSON: I'll do my best.

CLERK: And our examiners will be here in a moment.

JOHNSON: (*Who doesn't like the sound of this.*) What
examiners?

CLERK: For the usual preliminary questions. Meanwhile,
Mr Johnson, I advise you to take a good look at your
form.

(*He goes out. JOHNSON walks slowly to the chair at the
back of the desk, sits down and stares in bewilderment at the
pages of complicated questions. As he stares he pulls a pipe
out and sticks it into his mouth. Immediately.*)

VOICE FROM LOUD-SPEAKER: (*Severely.*) No smoking
in the office before five-fifteen.

(*After giving the loud-speaker a startled glance, JOHNSON
puts the pipe away. He tries to apply himself to the form, but
now the lights change, the ballet of clerks and secretaries
comes rushing in, making strange shadows, and we hear again
their strident nervous music. When these clerks and secretaries
have gone and the brilliant white lights pour down on the
desk again, we discover that the EXAMINERS have arrived,
and are standing one on each side of JOHNSON, who is still
seated. They are exactly alike, these EXAMINERS, tall and
rotund figures, dressed in frock-coats, with bald pink heads
and round pink shaven faces and large spectacles. They carry
notebooks. JOHNSON looks at them in astonishment touched
with horror, as well he might.*)

FIRST EXAMINER: (*Announcing himself.*) First Examiner.

SECOND EXAMINER: (*Announcing himself.*) Second
Examiner.

FIRST EXAMINER: Robert Johnson?

JOHNSON: Yes.

SECOND EXAMINER: (*Glancing at his notes.*) Born in
Grantham Street, Longfield?

JOHNSON: Yes.

FIRST EXAMINER: (*Reading from his notes.*) Elder son of
Frederick Johnson, solicitor's clerk, who for more than
ten years sacrificed a number of personal comforts and
pleasures in order to give you a good education?

JOHNSON: (*Staggered.*) Yes, I suppose he did. He – was a
good father.

SECOND EXAMINER: Did you ever thank him for those
sacrifices?

JOHNSON: (*Rather shamefaced.*) No. And I ought to have
done.

SECOND EXAMINER: (*Referring to his notes.*) Your
mother, Edith Johnson, I see, died of peritonitis at a
comparatively early age. She was warned that an
operation was necessary but refused to have one in time
because she was afraid of the expense and the trouble it
would cause her husband and children. You knew that, of
course?

JOHNSON: (*Deeply troubled.*) No – I didn't. I – I –
sometimes wondered – that's all.

FIRST EXAMINER: (*Glancing at his notebook, relentlessly.*)
And yet you have referred to yourself at times, I see, as a
good son.

JOHNSON: (*Thoroughly uncomfortable.*) I only meant – well
– we all seemed to get on together, y'know – not like
some families. They were very decent to me. I've always
admitted that. (*Hesitantly.*) As a matter of fact, I've been
thinking about all that…just lately… I remember, just
after I was taken ill –

SECOND EXAMINER: (*Briskly.*) Yes now – you were
taken ill.

JOHNSON: (*Brightening up, for we are all proud of our
illnesses.*) Yes. Quite suddenly. A most extraordinary
thing – but –

FIRST EXAMINER: (*Cutting in ruthlessly.*) You have
    occupied a responsible position for some time?

JOHNSON: (*Bewildered and rather sulky.*) Yes, I suppose so.

SECOND EXAMINER: (*Severely.*) You are a husband – and
    a father?

JOHNSON: Yes.

FIRST EXAMINER: (*Severely.*) What care have you taken
    of your health?

JOHNSON: (*Apologetically.*) Well – I've always tried –

FIRST EXAMINER: (*Ignoring him.*) The heart, the lungs,
    the liver and kidneys, the digestive system, the intestinal
    tract.

SECOND EXAMINER: The abdominal wall must be firm
    – no sagging.

FIRST EXAMINER: (*Who now sits on the desk, facing
    JOHNSON.*) The teeth need the greatest care. Particles of
    decaying food lodged in dental cavities may produce a
    septic condition.

SECOND EXAMINER: (*Also sitting.*) Eye-strain is common
    among sedentary workers. How often have you given
    yourself a boracic eye-bath or had your sight examined?

FIRST EXAMINER: Alcohol and rich starchy foods must
    be avoided. Have you avoided them?

SECOND EXAMINER: Smoking leads to nicotine
    poisoning and may easily ruin the digestion.

FIRST EXAMINER: Everywhere you go, you risk infection.

SECOND EXAMINER: But the common cold, the
    beginning of many serious ailments, may be traced to a
    lack of fresh air.

FIRST EXAMINER: Few of us take the trouble to walk
    properly.

SECOND EXAMINER: Or to sit properly. You should
    always sit upright, not allowing the spine to be curved.
    Learn to sit properly.
    (*The wretched JOHNSON, who has been slumped deep into
    his chair, now sharply raises himself to a more erect position,
    but it does not help him.*)

FIRST EXAMINER: But take care to relax. The nervous
    strain of modern life demands constant and complete
    relaxation. Loosen those tense muscles.

JOHNSON: (*Slumping again, but determined to protest at last.*) Now – look here – just a minute – !

SECOND EXAMINER: (*Very severely, rising.*) Please – we have no time to waste.

(*The two monsters make rapid and contemptuous notes in their books, while JOHNSON regards them helplessly.*)

FIRST EXAMINER: You owe it yourself, to your wife and family, to your employer and fellow workers, to your country, to take sufficient exercise.

JOHNSON: (*Who mistakenly feels on safer ground here.*) I've always enjoyed taking exercise. Tennis and golf –

SECOND EXAMINER: (*Very severely.*) Too many middle-aged men, sedentary workers, imagine they can improve their physical condition by rushing into games at the weekend, and only succeed in straining their hearts.

JOHNSON: (*Desperately.*) I've tried not to overdo it, and every morning, if I wasn't too late, I did a few exercises in my bedroom –

FIRST EXAMINER: (*Very severely.*) Nearly all systems of home exercises, devised by professional strong men without expert physical knowledge, are liable to do more harm than good.

SECOND EXAMINER: Consult your doctor first. *He* knows.

FIRST EXAMINER: But the habit of flying to the doctor on every trivial occasion is dangerous and must be avoided.

JOHNSON: (*Sinking fast now.*) Look here, gentlemen, all I can say is – I've tried to do my best.

SECOND EXAMINER: (*Going right up to him, in smooth deadly tone.*) Possibly. But is your best good enough?

FIRST EXAMINER: (*With the same horrible technique.*) After all, what do you *know*?

SECOND EXAMINER: (*Severe again now.*) How far have you tried to acquaint yourself with the findings of chemistry, physics, biology, geology, astronomy, mathematics?

FIRST EXAMINER: Ask yourself what you know about the Mendelian Law, the Quantum Theory, Spectral Analysis, or the behaviour of Electrons and Neutrons.

SECOND EXAMINER: Could you explain Freud's theory of the Id, Marx's Surplus Value, Neo-Realism, Non-representational Art, Polyphonic Music?

FIRST EXAMINER: Or – give an exact account of the sequence of events leading up to the outbreak of war in 1914?

SECOND EXAMINER: (*With dangerous easiness.*) You were taught French at school?

JOHNSON: Yes.

SECOND EXAMINER: (*Turning like a tiger.*) Have you ever brushed up your French?

JOHNSON: (*Desperately.*) No, but I've always been meaning to. Hang it – a man can't do everything!

FIRST EXAMINER: (*Calmly and maddeningly.*) A postman in South East London taught himself to speak eight foreign languages fluently in his spare time.

SECOND EXAMINER: (*In the same tone.*) A cinema operator in Pasadena, California, recently received an honours degree in natural sciences.

JOHNSON: (*Wearily, almost brokenly.*) I know, I know. And good luck to them. But as I told you –

FIRST EXAMINER: (*Very severely.*) Kindly tell us what we ask you to tell us. We have no time now for general conversation. You have two children?

JOHNSON: (*Brightening up, for this may let him out.*) Yes. A boy and a girl.

SECOND EXAMINER: You are fond of them?

JOHNSON: (*Indignantly.*) Of course I am.

FIRST EXAMINER: What serious thought have you ever given to their education, to their mental development, to their emotional and spiritual life?

SECOND EXAMINER: They are the citizens of the future, the inheritors of a great empire –

JOHNSON: I know, I know. I've often thought of that.

SECOND EXAMINER: (*Pressing him.*) Really thought about it, or merely, after an unnecessarily heavy meal accompanied by alcohol, congratulated yourself that these children were an extension of your own ego?

FIRST EXAMINER: You have helped to bring them into the world, but what kind of world have you brought them into?

JOHNSON: (*Hastily, hoping he is now on firmer ground.*) Oh
– well – I've no illusions about that.

SECOND EXAMINER: (*Angrily.*) We are not asking you
about your illusions. For many years now you have had a
vote?

JOHNSON: (*Still hoping.*) Yes, and I've always used it – not
like some chaps.

FIRST EXAMINER: But how much of your time and
serious attention have been given to the problems that
must be studied by a wise member of the electorate?

SECOND EXAMINER: For example, the Gold Standard as
against an artificial currency based on the balance of
trade. The relation between nationalism and Tariffs. The
fallacy of colonial exploitation.

FIRST EXAMINER: What account of any value could you
give of the political significance of minorities in Central
Europe, the importance of the Ukraine in European
affairs, the success or failure of Stalin's second Five Year
Plan?

SECOND EXAMINER: Could you define accurately
Fascism?

FIRST EXAMINER: National Socialism?

SECOND EXAMINER: Russian Communism?

JOHNSON: (*A rebel at last, jumping up.*) No. Could you?
(*As they do not reply, but make notes.*)
I might as well tell you, I've had enough of this. Who
are you, anyhow?
(*As they do not reply, but look at each other significantly.*)
I don't even know why I'm here. Loss of memory or
something. No reason why I should stay.

FIRST EXAMINER (*Ignoring this outburst.*) Your form,
please. (*He takes the form, hastily makes some remarks on it,
then hands it back.*)

JOHNSON: (*Angrily.*) I don't want the thing.
(*JOHNSON throws the form on the table and sits sulking.
The two EXAMINERS look at the form, then at him, give a
nod to each other, and go off through one of the big office
doors.*)
I'm not staying, y'know. Why should I? I didn't want to
come here. Keep your money.

(*But the EXAMINERS have gone. JOHNSON sits slumped in his chair behind the desk, a sulky rebel. And now the hard white lights go down, and a mysterious and rather ghastly light hovers over a small door that is not really in the office at all but much nearer to us, in fact in the false proscenium. There is one of these doors at each side of the false proscenium. Through this one, then, in the queer light enter the CLERK we have seen before and a miserable woman very poorly dressed. For a moment we do not recognise her as JILL JOHNSON.*)

CLERK: (*Indicating JOHNSON.*) Is that the man?

JILL: (*Who talks now in an angry whine.*) Yes, that's my husband.

JOHNSON: (*Astonished.*) Why – Jill!

JILL: (*Ignoring him.*) Yes, that's him. And look at him – doing nothing! And look at us – his wife and children – turned out of house and home – not a bite to eat all day. And why? Because my husband isn't man enough to do a decent day's work.

JOHNSON: (*Protesting.*) But Jill – I –

JILL: (*Shrilly, a virago now.*) Don't Jill me, Robert Johnson. I wish to God I'd never set eyes on you – and wish those poor children of mine – had never – never – been born. (*She is crying now, and as her voice dies away so she too seems to melt away. But the CLERK remains, to stare accusingly.*)

CLERK: (*In a large maddening tone.*) So that's the kind of man you are, is it, Johnson?

JOHNSON: (*Half bewildered, half angry.*) No, it isn't. I'm not like that at all. (*He goes down.*) Here – Jill. (*But JILL has disappeared several moments before and now the CLERK has gone and the light has changed. JOHNSON returns slowly and miserably to his seat behind the desk.*)

VOICE FROM LOUD-SPEAKER: All application forms to be completed within the next fifteen minutes. Only fifteen minutes more. (*But before JOHNSON can apply himself properly to the task of filling in the form, the irritating ballet of clerks and secretaries is back again, hiding JOHNSON from us and throwing gigantic shadows on the back wall. When they have gone and the hard white light is blazing away again, we discover that standing over JOHNSON is the SCHOOLMASTER he always disliked the most, the very same man wearing his chalky MA gown and mortar-board, and as of course he has come out of the past nearly forty years ago, he has a rather old-fashioned look. As soon as JOHNSON looks up, startled, to see this hateful figure, he becomes a sulky schoolboy again.)*

SCHOOLMASTER: (*One of those sarcastic fellows.*) You'll not be terribly surprised to learn, Johnson, that I'm not pleased with you.

JOHNSON: (*Raising a schoolboy hand.*) Honestly – sir – it's not my fault. You see –

SCHOOLMASTER: No excuses, please, Johnson. I hear too many, and I've been hearing them for thirty-five years, and yours are among the worst I've ever heard. Now – if it isn't boring you, Johnson, for I know how easily bored you become – might I ask, as a special favour, if you remember a certain wise saw I am in the habit of repeating?

JOHNSON: (*Who loathes the thing.*) Attention to work is the secret of progress.

SCHOOLMASTER: Right. Attention to work is the secret of progress. But your trouble, Johnson, is that you don't attend to work. You don't seem to attend to anything very much, these days, do you? Mr Morrison tells me he's dropping you out of the House Eleven because you won't attend even there. No doubt you're busy on the playing field thinking about the work you ought to have done for me.

JOHNSON: (*Who feels there is something in this.*) Well, sir, honestly it is a *bit* like that –

SCHOOLMASTER: I said no excuses, Johnson. And now, just to make sure you *do* attend to something for once, you'll spend the rest of this afternoon writing me an essay on the causes of the Thirty Years War.

JOHNSON: Oh but – sir – !

SCHOOLMASTER: (*Firmly.*) The causes of the Thirty Years War, thank you, Johnson.

(*He sweeps out majestically. JOHNSON, still the schoolboy, looks in that direction and makes a rude face and a rude noise. We can just hear him muttering to himself.*)

JOHNSON: Old pig! Thirty Years War – oh – golly! Causes of the Thirty Years War.

(*But then as he stares at the table in front of him, he is first puzzled and then relieved, suddenly remembering that he is not a schoolboy any longer. No, he certainly isn't a schoolboy, but how far does that take him? What is he now? We can see him asking himself these questions, still bewildered.*)

VOICE FROM LOUD-SPEAKER: All applicants with forms still not completed must hurry now. Only a few minutes left.

(*As JOHNSON tries to settle down with his form again, two typical NEWSPAPER BOYS come hurrying on, one at each side of the desk, and begin calling out in their usual style.*)

FIRST NEWSPAPER BOY: All abou' the big dee-saster.

SECOND NEWSPAPER BOY: All abou' the 'orrible mur-der.

FIRST NEWSPAPER BOY: All abou' the Cri-sis.

SECOND NEWSPAPER BOY: All abou' the fall o' Peking, Barcelona, Madrid.

FIRST NEWSPAPER BOY: All abou' the end o' Rome, Vienna, Berlin, Paris.

SECOND NEWSPAPER BOY: All abou' the burning o' London.

FIRST NEWSPAPER BOY: All abou' the Great Plague.

SECOND NEWSPAPER BOY: All abou' the end o' the world.

(*Up to the last two or three cries, JOHNSON has resisted them, but now he comes forward, putting a hand in his pocket for coppers, feeling very anxious.*)

JOHNSON: Here, what's all this?

FIRST NEWSPAPER BOY: (*Coolly.*) All the winners.

SECOND NEWSPAPER BOY: (*Hopefully.*) Duke stung by wasp.

JOHNSON: (*Annoyed.*) Go on. Clear out.

(*They hurry out. JOHNSON returns to the desk and starts on the form again, but the music begins and a solitary clerk-*

dancer appears and performs his antics just in front of where JOHNSON is sitting. JOHNSON rises angrily.)

(*Shouting.*) Oh – for God's sake – stop that. Get out – and stay out.

(*He takes a few menacing steps towards the clerk, who hurries out, through one of the office doors. The light changes, the desk no longer being brilliantly illuminated, and, in a more normal light, MR CLAYTON strides in through one of the small proscenium doors. He is at least twenty-five years younger than he was when we last saw him in the hall of JOHNSON's house, and of course he is dressed like a prosperous City man of the pre-War period. He is extremely angry.)*

CLAYTON: (*Shouting.*) Johnson!

JOHNSON: (*Turning round, surprised.*) Why – Mr Clayton!

CLAYTON: (*Angrily.*) You young idiot, you were distinctly told to send out all those invoices dated the thirtieth.

JOHNSON: (*Now a dismayed junior clerk again.*) No – I wasn't, sir.

CLAYTON: You were. I told you myself, a week ago. Every invoice to be dated the thirtieth. We shall have to send every customer an apology, and you can begin writing them now and stay until they're done. If you'd think a little more about your work and less about the Alhambra and the Oval, we wouldn't have these idiotic mistakes. And if this occurs again, Johnson, you'd better go and amuse yourself in some other office.

JOHNSON: (*Very apologetically.*) Honestly, Mr Clayton, it wasn't my fault.

CLAYTON: (*As he bangs out.*) Rubbish!

(*As JOHNSON stands near the door through which CLAYTON has just gone, and as he stares at it, puzzled and depressed, through the other small door MRS GREGG enters quickly and quietly and sits down on the settee in front of the desk. She is now about forty-five, and dressed in the fashion of twenty-five years ago. She is doing some sewing.)*

MRS GREGG: (*Quietly, but firmly.*) You'd better come here, Robert, and talk to me.

JOHNSON: (*Turning, surprised.*) Why, Mrs Gregg! (*He goes nearer nervously.*) Did – er – Jill – tell you?

MRS GREGG: She did. And I do think it would have been much better if you had spoken to me first yourself, Robert. You must remember I am in a very difficult position, for I have to be both father and mother to poor Jill now.

JOHNSON: (*Sitting by her, awkwardly.*) Well, I'm sorry, Mrs Gregg. I didn't know quite what to do –

MRS GREGG: Of course Jill thinks it's all very wonderful, but the poor child's very young and has had no experience.

JOHNSON: (*Eagerly, the young lover.*) I'll make her happy, I know I will.

MRS GREGG: (*Primly.*) We've never been wealthy, of course, but before my husband's death we were reasonably well off, and I think you ought to understand that Jill has been used to a great deal more than you can possibly offer her for a long time. I've no personal objection to you, Robert, though frankly I had hoped that Jill would do much better for herself. What can *you* offer her?

JOHNSON: (*Unhappily, for what can he offer her?*) Well, I know I'm no great catch –

MRS GREGG: (*Closing her eyes, primly.*) There's no need to be vulgar, Robert.

JOHNSON: Sorry. But – really – I don't think my prospects are too bad.

MRS GREGG: (*Putting her sewing together.*) If you'll come to tea on Sunday, Jill's uncle, my brother, will be there – he's a solicitor and understands business – and then perhaps you wouldn't mind answering a few questions and telling him exactly what you think your prospects are. Four on Sunday, then, Robert.
(*And out she goes, leaving JOHNSON staring after her miserably, for apparently he knows this uncle, and we hear him muttering.*)

JOHNSON: Lord! He'll never understand, that hard old devil. Make me look like tuppence. Nice Sunday we're going to have. Prospects!
(*He sits down, still the young lover, perhaps to make a few notes on his prospects, then he sees the form in front of him,*)

slowly recognises it, and the twenty-five years that have elapsed since he had that little talk with MRS GREGG vanish again in a flash.)

VOICE FROM LOUD-SPEAKER: All applicants must now complete their forms by answering the question they are considering.

JOHNSON: (*Reading from his form.*) If you had lent your brother ten pounds when you were twenty, and you now compelled him to return the loan with compound interest at fifteen per cent, what would he pay you? (*After a pause.*) That oughtn't to be hard. (*Pauses again.*) But why should I work it out? I wouldn't charge my brother compound interest or any other interest. Why ask such a question? And how did they know I had a brother? Perhaps they mean any brother. They say in church we're all brothers. That's awkward.

(And now he hears – and we hear too – some music of a kind we have not heard here yet but will hear later when we come to the Inn. JOHNSON listens to it, then speaks slowly, as if an inner and deeper self is talking.)

That music doesn't belong to this place. But then neither do I. Who does? I've lived in the world where that music was, but not for long – no, never for long. Not my fault. It comes and goes so quickly, just gleams and fades, that other world, like the light at sunset on distant hills…

(The music goes on, high and trailing, but now a girl's voice sings with it, high and trailing too. He listens a moment before speaking.)

But perhaps that is real – that, somewhere outside – and this only a dream. I've had dreams like this – with everything at first solid as rock – though they tell us now rocks aren't solid, only shifting shapes – but afterwards it all melted away, all the stone walls and iron bars… (*This reminds him of something as he repeats it.*) Stone walls – iron bars… (*He looks up to see approaching a pale wretched young man in convict's dress and behind him a stalwart POLICEMAN. The two of them move slowly down and halt in front of JOHNSON, who starts up and comes round as he recognises the CONVICT.*)

Why – Charlie – yes, it is!

CONVICT: (*In dead tone.*) Yes, Johnson, it's me all right.

JOHNSON: (*Amazed and distressed.*) But – they said – you'd died there – in prison.

CONVICT: If you ask me, I died that afternoon in the dock, *you* remember. Yes, that's when I really died.

JOHNSON: Charlie, I'm sorry. You don't know how sorry I've been, how often I've thought about it all.

CONVICT: (*With a miserable sneer.*) *Thought* about it!

JOHNSON: (*Distressed.*) But what could we do, Charlie, what could we do? They dragged the evidence out of us. We didn't want to make it hard for you, Charlie. And afterwards we tried to do what we could.

CONVICT: What could you do?

JOHNSON: There wasn't much, I know. They wouldn't let us send you anything, but some of us clubbed together to give the girl something.

CONVICT: (*Loudly and angrily.*) Give the girl something! All she wanted was me, and where did you put me?

POLICEMAN: (*Roughly.*) Go on, you, and not so much talk. (*The CONVICT, without another look at JOHNSON, continues on his way across, while the POLICEMAN, after following him a few paces, suddenly stops and turns, to address JOHNSON.*)

(*Heavily.*) And listen, mister, *you* be careful.

JOHNSON: (*Stammering.*) What – what – do you mean?

POLICEMAN: (*Severely.*) I mean, be careful, that's all. Don't think we haven't had our eye on *you.*

JOHNSON: (*Protesting, though at once feeling guilty.*) But – I've never done anything.

POLICEMAN: (*Aggressively.*) Oh! Well, let's see. (*Produces notebook, and adopts manner of police witness.*) Did or did you not, on the first of the fifth, 1906, take two shillings' worth of stamps out of the stamp book at your office?

JOHNSON: (*Staggered.*) Well – yes, I did.

POLICEMAN: (*Significantly.*) Ah!

JOHNSON: (*Hurriedly protesting.*) But I was only a youngster – gave way to sudden temptation – I was hard up and wanted to buy something in a hurry – and I put two shillings in stamps back the next day – I –

POLICEMAN: (*Same manner as before.*) Did you or did you not – on several occasions – make tax returns you knew at the time were false – ?

JOHNSON: (*Trying to cut in.*) I only –

POLICEMAN: (*Checking him.*) Did you or did you not – in connection with a large order from Singapore, when a higher price was quoted by mistake, and you was on the point of cabling your customer the proper price – accept this large order at the higher price and cancel the cable?

JOHNSON: Well, I was doing it for the firm.

POLICEMAN: Did you or did you not – on the third of the eleventh, 1931, deliberately hide one of the firm's books – to keep it from the accountants for a day or two – ?

JOHNSON: (*Desperately.*) We were in a temporary difficulty – and I –

POLICEMAN: (*Interrupting, severely.*) Tell *me* you've never done anything! Get yourself into *serious* trouble one of these days. Don't think we haven't got our eye on you. Be careful, that's all. Just be careful.

(*He gives poor JOHNSON a final severe look, then goes out. JOHNSON sinks down on to the settee in front of the desk, and looks down at the form he is still holding.*)

JOHNSON: (*Reading.*) Just before the outbreak of war, you have bought up all the available stocks of iodine. You can either let the wholesalers have some at an increased price, or go to the department of medical supplies and name your own price. Which would be wiser? (*He looks at it horrified.*) Wiser?

(*The lights change, and the clerks and secretaries flicker about, while JOHNSON remains motionless, silent and depressed. When they have gone, and the bright lights are back again, we see that the EXAMINERS are standing one at each side of him.*)

FIRST EXAMINER: (*Announcing himself.*) First Examiner.

SECOND EXAMINER: (*Announcing himself.*) Second Examiner.

FIRST EXAMINER: Your form, please.

SECOND EXAMINER: (*Looking at it.*) Miserable!

FIRST EXAMINER: Contemptible!

SECOND EXAMINER: He's hardly tried.

FIRST EXAMINER: (*Screwing up the form.*) We couldn't possibly accept this.

SECOND EXAMINER: No money for you this time. (*Both EXAMINERS move away, then turn.*)

FIRST EXAMINER: You'll have to try again tomorrow. Keep on trying.

SECOND EXAMINER: Try, try, and try again.

JOHNSON: (*Sullenly.*) I'm not going to try again, and I'm not coming here tomorrow.

FIRST EXAMINER: (*Cackling.*) No, you're not *coming* here tomorrow because you'll still *be* here tomorrow.

JOHNSON: (*Defiantly.*) I won't.

SECOND EXAMINER: (*Cackling.*) But you forget that without money you can't get out of here…

FIRST EXAMINER: You needn't pay any money to get out, but you must have money.

SECOND EXAMINER: And you haven't any. You wouldn't be here if you had.

(*JOHNSON is slumped in despair on the settee. The two EXAMINERS move together nearer the door, then turn again, and now in their tones are horrible echoes of the SCHOOLMASTER and CLAYTON and MRS GREGG.*)

FIRST EXAMINER: Try again tomorrow, Johnson. Keep on trying.

SECOND EXAMINER: Remember, Johnson, attention to work is the secret of progress.

FIRST EXAMINER: Think more about your work, Johnson.

SECOND EXAMINER: Ask yourself exactly what your prospects are.

FIRST EXAMINER: (*In a nasty little squeak, to the music.*) Good day.

SECOND EXAMINER: (*In the same manner.*) Good day. (*Out they go together, and now the brilliant lights begin to fade. JOHNSON is still slumped on the settee. The very brisk strident music heard before is now a sort of broken dragging march in a minor key. The lights go down further.*)

VOICE FROM LOUD-SPEAKER: Everything for the incinerators. Everything for the incinerators.

(The clerks come on, carrying baskets filled with paper, spilling some of the paper as they move slowly towards the back, where a curtain lifts showing a gleaming red opening. A tall FIGURE is standing there, with his back to us, dressed in workman's clothes, and his job appears to be to feed the furnace with the baskets of paper. We can see him easily above the great desk because he is standing on a little platform, at one side of which there is a flight of steps leading we do not know where. As the clerks go off, rather like pieces of clockwork running down, JOHNSON rises, as the music ends, and picks up one or two of the nearest bits of paper.)

JOHNSON: *(Excitedly.)* Why – this is money. What are you going to do with it?

VOICE FROM LOUD-SPEAKER: *(Coolly.)* Burn it. Everything has to go to the incinerators at the end of the day.

JOHNSON: Yes – but – money too?

VOICE FROM LOUD-SPEAKER: Yes, money too. All the same.

JOHNSON: *(With mounting excitement.)* But – I want some money.

(He is looking up towards the loud-speakers, but as no reply comes from them, now he goes nearer the FIGURE, who still has his back turned to us, feeding the furnace. JOHNSON now addresses the FIGURE.)

I say – look here – silly to burn all that money, when I want some.

THE FIGURE: *(Not turning.)* How much?

JOHNSON: *(Very excited now.)* How much? Well, much as I can get, I suppose. And it looks to me as if these are banknotes – and big ones, some of 'em.

THE FIGURE: Yes.

JOHNSON: Well, now, couldn't I have a few? Say, a handful? A pocketful? Two pockets full? *All* my pockets full? Could I?

THE FIGURE: *(In deep mocking tone.)* Come and get it. *(As he says this, the FIGURE turns round, holding out money, but revealing himself, to the sound of harsh menacing brassy chords from the orchestra, wearing a terrifying death's head.*

He stands in a queer deathly light, on the steps, a foot or two above JOHNSON, who has now mounted the platform. We can see nothing now but these two, and the red gleam of the furnace.)

(As JOHNSON does not move, mockingly.) Well, come and get it. Frightened?

JOHNSON: *(As he shrinks back.)* Yes.

THE FIGURE: Why?

JOHNSON: *(Slowly, unhappily.)* I always have been. It's been behind everything, waiting – that fear. The dark grave, corruption, and the worm. I remember, when I was a child, seeing the half-rotten carcase of a cat, white and crawling with maggots. Then once, the swollen purple face of a drowned man. Then later, my mother, smiling but turned into wax; a sickly sweet smell all over the house; the heavy tread of the coffin bearers; the thudding of the clay on the coffin lid. I went to the War and I remember the vacant eye-sockets of my dead friends. There was a hand I have tried to forget. It was sticking out of a parapet, a mute and rigid cry for help, as if the rest of him had been turned into earth and sandbags, and he knew – he still knew – and held out a hand towards the warm living flesh, before the worms were at us too – oh God! –

THE FIGURE: *(Calmly.)* The worms are God's, too. Why shouldn't they have their chance?

JOHNSON: *(Bitterly.)* Theirs is a better chance. They do not know what is waiting for them – we do.

THE FIGURE: You have been afraid so long, there cannot be anything left to fear. Come. *(He holds out the money.)*

JOHNSON: *(Shuddering.)* No.

THE FIGURE: *(Sharply.)* Come and look closer, you fool. Come.

(Now, very slowly, as if drawn against his will, JOHNSON moves closer, and then within a pace or two, stops and stares.)

JOHNSON: Why – it's a mask, a painted mask.

(He goes a little nearer to make sure, while the FIGURE stands upright, still waiting, a whole sack of money in front of him.)

THE FIGURE: Take it off.

JOHNSON: (*Fearfully.*) No. There might be worse behind it. Death's real face – not even the clean bone – a crawling corruption –

THE FIGURE: You will be here for ever if you don't.

[*JOHNSON hesitates, then, making up his mind, he suddenly steps forward, as the music makes a queer high tremolo, and plucks off the mask, revealing behind it the face of a calm, wise-looking person, at whom JOHNSON stares in bewilderment.*]

(*Apparently amused.*) Well?

JOHNSON: (*Slowly.*) You are like – and yet not quite like – so many people I have known. It's as if they all looked at me together. My father...our old family doctor, MacFarlane...and my first schoolmaster...even our old nurse...and a parson I once talked to, just one night, crossing to France...and...and...

(*He cannot at the moment think of any more, but he knows and we know there are probably hundreds more.*)

THE FIGURE: (*Calmly.*) Do you still want your money?

JOHNSON: (*Eagerly and with an unpleasant swagger.*) Yes of course I do. Lucky I had the guts to take off that foul mask, wasn't it? But I'm not bad when it comes to a real push. Put me really up against it, and I don't disgrace myself. Yes, let's have some money, and get out of this. (*As he fills his pockets with notes.*) Fivers, tenners, and I saw a hundred-pound note. This is something to be going on with, eh? I can do something with this packet. And nobody can say I haven't earned it, can they?

(*While he is stuffing the last of the notes into his pockets, what seemed before the small opening down to a furnace is now revealed as a decorated and brightly illuminated corridor, and along this corridor comes the sound of a dance band.*)

Listen! What's that music? Sounds good to me.

THE FIGURE: Oh – that! It's the night club – the *Jungle Hot Spot.* Bright lights. Hot Jazz. Dinners, suppers, drinks, beautiful girls.

JOHNSON: They'll take this money there, eh?

THE FIGURE: They'll be delighted to take it.

JOHNSON: That's the place for me then. Let's have some fun while we're alive, I say; we're a long time dead. What do you say?

THE FIGURE: (*Rather sadly.*) I say what I've always said, Robert, that there isn't much harm in you, but nevertheless you're rather a fool.

JOHNSON: (*Angrily.*) Oh yes, that's just what you *would* say. Just when I look like having some fun for once, you'd like to butt in and spoil everything. Well, you're not going to this time. I'm going to see what's going on in this hot spot of yours.

(*The entrance to the night club is now brighter than ever and the dance music is growing louder. JOHNSON is now shouting with excitement.*)

That's the stuff, boys. Come on, snap into it. Keep it going, and make it hot. We'll have a big night. I'm coming.

He waves a hand and down he goes, out of sight, and the dance music is louder than ever and the curtain is falling.

ACT TWO

*We are looking again at the hall of JOHNSON's house, but now it is
the afternoon of the day following the funeral, and the place does not
look quite so dreary as it did before. AGNES is arranging some
flowers on the small table, and now FREDA, wearing an overall
and still looking rather peaked, comes out of the drawing-room,
carrying some wilted large lilies.*

FREDA: Agnes, take these and throw them out.

AGNES: (*As she takes the lilies.*) Yes, miss. Though they're
not done yet, not by a long way. If you was to cut their
stalks –

FREDA: No, I hate them. Big sickly lilies. I think it was the
sight of them yesterday that started me off.

AGNES: I thought you got through it very well, Miss
Freda.

FREDA: No, I didn't, Agnes. I was stupid.
(*RICHARD, wearing an overcoat, comes in, and stops at the
hall-stand to leave his hat and overcoat there. AGNES goes
out with the lilies. FREDA, who has taken over the job of
arranging the flowers, stops and turns when she hears her
brother coming in. We can have a good look at them now, and
see that they make a pleasant pair of youngsters.*)
Oh – Richard – what was it like?

RICHARD: A bit mouldy. Then old Clayton came in, and
told me to pop off. He's coming here tomorrow – he and
Uncle George, to settle things. How's Mother?

FREDA: (*Not very happily.*) Just the same. Very, very quiet –
and sort of strange –

RICHARD: (*Uneasily.*) It would be better – wouldn't it – if
she was making a fuss – you know, crying – ?

FREDA: Much. This other thing's a bit – frightening.

RICHARD: I know. Where is she?

FREDA: Upstairs. She said she'd lie down. (*She pauses.*) Do
you think – he knows?

RICHARD: Who?

FREDA: Daddy, of course.

RICHARD: Knows what?

FREDA: (*Very earnestly.*) Knows that all this has been going on – all that awful fuss yesterday and then this strange quietness today?

RICHARD: No, of course not. When you're dead, you're dead.

FREDA: Yes, but you might know what was going on?

RICHARD: Don't be a chump. How *could* you?

FREDA: I don't know, but I feel somehow you might.

RICHARD: Why, he didn't know anything that last two days. Just muttered a bit, that's all. In a sort of dream, really.

FREDA: (*Who has been thinking about this.*) Well, supposing the dreaming goes on. Then you wouldn't even know you'd died, would you? And then it wouldn't be so bad for him as it is for us – would it? I mean, because he could be dreaming about still being with us, and wouldn't really know the difference.

RICHARD: (*Thoughtfully.*) He would. You always do in dreams. There's something queer about them. You always know. (*Pause.*) All today I've been thinking about him. Couldn't stop, somehow. Y'know, Freda, I was a bit rotten to him sometimes. Didn't mean to be. It was all right when I was a kid – we had some grand times – but just lately he began to think I was getting too cheeky and I thought he interfered too much, as if I was still a kid – you know how it was.

FREDA: Yes.

RICHARD: (*Slowly.*) I thought I'd tell him it was all right and I was sorry and all that, but it was too late then – he couldn't understand what anybody was saying to him.

FREDA: Perhaps if you thought it, he got it somehow. (*Pause.*) You know, I used to think of him as being quite old.

RICHARD: Lord yes! So did I. Terribly old.

FREDA: I know. Well, just lately I've suddenly seen he isn't really old – I mean – (*She is distressed.*) – he wasn't. (*Her mother, JILL, now comes in slowly, a pale-faced figure in black, looking almost as if she were walking in her sleep.*)

FREDA: (*Turning, reproachfully.*) Oh – mother – you said you were going to rest.

JILL: (*Apologetically.*) I know, darling.

FREDA: Agnes and I can do everything. There isn't much
more to do.

RICHARD: And I'll help, Come on, mother, let me take
you back to your room. Then try and sleep.

JILL: (*With suppressed agitation.*) No, darling. I did try. I was
– half asleep. Then I had a hateful sort of dream.
Frightening, horrible. I suppose it was really a
nightmare. I dreamt I was trying to find your father. I
knew I had to find him. And I had to look in the
strangest places – all vague – but – frightening –
(*By the time she has said the last word the light, which has
been fading rapidly, has almost gone, and the next moment
we are in darkness… At first we do not see all the night club
but only the bar, a small cocktail bar, gaudily decorated,
glittering, and lit with strange crimson and purple lights.
JOHNSON, now in full evening dress, is perched on a stool,
swallowing cocktails and talking to the BARMAN, a smooth,
white-coated, rather sinister fellow. JOHNSON is already
beginning to feel the effect of the cocktails.*)

JOHNSON: What do you call this? (*Holds up brightly
coloured cocktail.*)

BARMAN: Hell Diver, sir.

JOHNSON: Hell Diver, eh?

BARMAN: One of my specialities.

JOHNSON: (*After gulping it down.*) I like it better than the
blue one. What do you call the blue one?

BARMAN: Mermaid's kiss.

JOHNSON: Pretty good. But this Hell Diver is better.
Touches the spot, eh? Let me have another.
(*As BARMAN begins mixing another.*)
Now, where have those nice fellows gone? I hope they
didn't pay you for those drinks.

BARMAN: (*Smoothly.*) No, sir, they said you were paying.

JOHNSON: (*Drinking.*) Quite right, quite right. What's the
name of that smart, clever-looking one, who said he
could put me on to something?

BARMAN: Probably Mr Scorpion, sir, One of our regular
customers here, sir. Here every night, nearly.

JOHNSON: (*Drinking.*) Quite right. I shall come here every night. And what was the little gentleman's name – that legal man in the City?

BARMAN: Mr Rat, sir. Comes here a lot with Mr Slug. You were talking to Mr Slug.

JOHNSON: (*With fussy importance.*) Yes, yes. Had very interesting talk with Mr Slug. Nice crowd.
(*As BARMAN hands him a bright yellow drink.*)
What's this one?

BARMAN: Dragon's Breath.

JOHNSON: Always wanted to try a Dragon's Breath. (*Gulps it, gasps, then tosses BARMAN a note.*) Keep the change.

BARMAN: There isn't any change, sir. With all the drinks together your bill comes to –

JOHNSON: (*Cutting in.*) All right. Don't want any arithmetic tonight. (*Tosses him another note.*) Keep the change out of *that*.

BARMAN: (*Not impressed.*) Thanks.

JOHNSON: (*More to himself than to the BARMAN.*) Man needs a little recreation. Relax. Can't be solemn and responsible all the time. Not good enough. Bad for a fellow, too, not to hit the bright lights and hot spots once in a while. Scorpion and Slug were quite right. Good enough for them, good enough for me.
(*Now JOHNSON leaves the bar and comes towards us, and we no longer see the bar but only JOHNSON's face, strained with excitement in the sharp white light.*)
(*With mounting excitement.*) There is a beast with shaggy hide and claws, and now he has roused himself from his long sleep, and I feel his fiery breath. Now I begin to see with his eyes and hear with his ears, and the lights burn terribly and the sounds pulsate through my blood.
(*He turns, and immediately the floor of the night club comes into view and we hear the music of a rumba and see a number of well-dressed but rather unpleasant-looking people dancing. There are little tables and chairs round the dance floor, and at the back, under a large decoration made of glittering writhing tinsel leaves, is a small platform. The scene is lit with acid greens and violent purples. JOHNSON regards it with enthusiasm.*)

Just the sort of place I wanted. Couldn't be better. Make a big night of it.

(*The dance has ended and now the bar is lit up again, and there enter from below SIR JAMES PORKER, a fat grunting elderly man, and two GIRLS, who look exactly alike, chiefly because they are wearing masks like dolls' faces. JOHNSON stares at them curiously.*)

BARMAN: Good evening, Sir James.

PORKER: (*Grunting.*) Evening. Gimme three of the usual.

BARMAN: Three of the usual.

(*As PORKER and his two GIRLS settle at the bar, the HEADWAITER, a plump smooth foreign fellow with a queer face, comes down and bows.*)

HEADWAITTER: (*Bowing.*) Good evening, Sir James. A great pleasure, Sir James. Good evening, ladies.

PORKER: 'Evening, Toad. Got my table?

HEADWAITER: Certainly, Sir James. Any time you are ready. You would like to see the menu, Sir James?

PORKER: (*Who never experiments.*) No. Gimme all the usual.

HEADWAITER: (*Bowing.*) Certainly, Sir James – all the usual.

(*PORKER and the GIRLS now have their drinks. The HEADWAITER notices the existence of JOHNSON, who has been hovering not far away, waiting to be noticed.*)

Good evening, sir. You will be wanting a table?

JOHNSON: (*Vaguely, but grandly.*) Oh – yes. Table – certainly.

HEADWAITER: For how many please, sir?

JOHNSON: Oh – I dunno. Pick somebody up, I expect.

HEADWAITER: Of course, sir. Lots of charr-ming ladies will be here soon.

(*He tries to lead JOHNSON away, to a table, but JOHNSON resists this and brings him further down.*)

JOHNSON: (*Whispering.*) Does it matter not being in evening dress?

HEADWAITER: (*Surprised.*) But, sir, you are quite all right.

(*He indicates JOHNSON's clothes. JOHNSON looks down and is obviously surprised by what he sees and clearly did not know he was in evening clothes.*)

JOHNSON: (*Slowly, puzzled.*) That's queer. I wasn't wearing these.

HEADWAITER: You must have changed in a great hurry, sir. Now will give you a good table.

JOHNSON: (*Importantly.*) One of your very best.

HEADWAITER: Certainly, sir, one of our very best.

JOHNSON: (*Vulgarly.*) What I always say is – the best is good enough for me.

HEADWAITER: (*A diplomat.*) Oh – very well put, sir. I must remember that. Now, sir – (*Leading him towards a table.*) Some supper – a little wine, eh? – dancing – and a nice girl, eh, sir?

JOHNSON: (*As he sits down.*) That's the idea. Enjoy yourself while you can, I say.

HEADWAITER: Quite right, sir.

JOHNSON: (*Pleased with himself.*) Eat, drink and be merry, eh?

HEADWAITER: Excellent, sir. And very well put, if I may say so.

JOHNSON: Let's live while we can, I say, because we're a long time dead.

HEADWAITER: (*With faintly sinister inflection.*) Exactly, sir. A long time dead. I must remember that too, sir.

JOHNSON: (*Going from bad to worse.*) I have the money – (*And he shows a roll of notes.*) – And I've earned it – so I'll do what I like with it. And I can spend it – you'll see that. Give me a good time – and I'll see you're all right.

HEADWAITER: We will give you a very good time, sir. (*Now he bends forward and indicates PORKER, who is sitting with his GIRLS at a table opposite, loaded with food.*) (*Whispering.*) You know that gentleman? Very rich, one of our best patrons, always here. Sir James Porker.

JOHNSON: (*Looking across.*) He looks the right sort. (*PORKER, seeing that JOHNSON is looking across at him with interest, now waves a hand and beckons JOHNSON to him. Flattered by this notice, JOHNSON goes across.*)

PORKER: (*Talking with his mouth full.*) 'Evening. Seem to know your face.

JOHNSON: (*Pleased.*) My name's Johnson. And you're Sir James Porker, I think.

65

PORKER: Right. Come here a lot. Know the girls? This is
Dot. This is Maisie.

JOHNSON: (*Smiling idiotically.*) How d'you do?

PORKER: In the City?

JOHNSON: Yes.

PORKER: Might put you on to a good thing one of these
days. Still plenty of good things if you know where to
find 'em and get in on the ground floor.

JOHNSON: (*Impressed.*) Thanks very much.

PORKER: (*As dancing begins again.*) Like to dance, Johnson?

JOHNSON: Yes. But I need a partner.

PORKER: Dot here'll dance with you.

(*JOHNSON bows to DOT and begins dancing with her, He
dances with enthusiasm but not with much skill, occasionally
bumping into other couples. We hear what he is saying to his
partner.*)

JOHNSON: This is fine… Hope you're enjoying it? Long
time since I danced with such a pretty girl… Like
dancing too, but a bit out of practice – busy man,
y'know… A man's as old as he feels, I always say. What
do *you* think? …Like your hair – wonderful hair you've
got. Expect a lot of fellows have told you that, but after
all the opinion of a man of the world's worth having, eh?
(*When the dancing ends, he takes her back to PORKER's
table and stands there a minute or two.*)

PORKER: (*Patronisingly.*) Enjoy your dance, Johnson?

JOHNSON: Oh yes – delightful!

PORKER: Dot's a good dancer. Sometimes take her round
myself. Maisie here talks better.

JOHNSON: (*Glancing at her.*) Oh – really!

PORKER: Yes. Says some pretty smart things sometimes.
Makes yer laugh. But Dot knows the best stories – very
juicy.

JOHNSON: (*Coarsely.*) Oh – I like 'em juicy.

PORKER: (*Very suggestively.*) And that isn't all they can do,
not by a long chalk. Is it, girls? I'll say it isn't. Eh,
Johnson?

(*He guffaws and JOHNSON guffaws with him, and then
JOHNSON turns away and sees a STOUT WOMAN,
middle-aged, standing in the bar, which is now lit up again,*)

beckoning to him. This woman is very elaborately dressed, but has a coarse leering quality. JOHNSON joins her in the bar. The rest of the night club is now in darkness.)

STOUT WOMAN: (*With a leer.*) You don't remember me, do you?

JOHNSON: (*Who doesn't.*) Er – let me see – now –

STOUT WOMAN: Weren't you once little Bobby Johnson, Grantham Street, Longfield?

JOHNSON: (*Surprised.*) Why – yes –

STOUT WOMAN: (*Chuckling.*) Knew it! And you don't remember me? When I was a kid. Lived next door but one. Lottie Spragg.

JOHNSON: (*Staring at her in wonder.*) Of course! Lottie Spragg. Yes, of course.

STOUT WOMAN: (*In obscene whisper.*) Remember how all you boys used to take me behind the old mill?

JOHNSON: Oh – I don't think I did –

STOUT WOMAN: (*In the same tone.*) Go on, you was as bad as the rest of 'em. Naughty little devils! Do you remember –

(*As she leans forward to whisper, the lights go down in the bar, though JOHNSON and the woman can still be seen there, and now a single white ray picks out JILL who has just entered below, on the other side. She looks exactly as we saw her when she came into the hall to tell the children about her dream. The music is playing softly.*)

JILL: (*Urgently.*) I'm looking for my husband, Robert Johnson.

(*Two dancers turn in the light that follows her, and she sees – and we see – that they are wearing horrible masks, which turn them into dreadful caricatures of the types who might be found in such a place. She shrinks away, then moves on.*) (*More urgently.*) I'm looking for my husband, Robert Johnson.

(*As she goes forward, she sees more masked dancers, and then she stops near a group, consisting of the HEADWAITER and two or three ordinary waiters, and as she speaks again, they all turn together, and we see that they look more like animals than human beings.*)

(*Calling.*) Robert! Robert! Robert!

(*We catch a last glimpse of her surrounded by horrible masked figures, gibbering and tittering. Now JOHNSON stops the STOUT WOMAN a moment and looks up, as if hearing something.*)

JOHNSON: (*Calling, in hard voice.*) He's not here. Go away. Go away.

(*The light that was on JILL has now faded out, but in the darkness we still hear a faint and dying 'Robert! Robert!' Then the bar is bright again and JOHNSON and the STOUT WOMAN are laughing together.*)

STOUT WOMAN: (*Chuckling and nudging him.*) Saucy devil! You're just as bad as ever. So am I.

JOHNSON: Ah – but we know a bit more now.

STOUT WOMAN: (*Still chuckling.*) Well, we started as we meant to go on, didn't we? (*Moving.*) I must get back to the boys. Don't do anything I wouldn't do. Happy days!

JOHNSON: (*As he takes her down.*) Happy nights, you mean. So long!

(*When she has gone and he turns to the bar again, he finds installed there on a stool the young man CHARLIE, whom we saw in the office as a convict. But now apparently CHARLIE did not get found out, for he is very spruce indeed in full evening dress and with a carnation as a buttonhole, and he is obviously very much at home in this bar.*)

CHARLIE: Well, if it's not old stick-in-the-mud Johnson!

JOHNSON: Charlie? Yes, it is.

CHARLIE: (*To BARMAN.*) Two of my specials, George. These'll put hair on your chest, Johnson. Well, how's tricks?

JOHNSON: (*Sitting.*) Fine, fine, absolutely fine. You're looking very prosperous, Charlie.

CHARLIE: (*In the close, confidential bar-style of such men.*) You bet I am. I had a nice little start with that fifteen hundred I pinched right from under old Clayton's nose. Neatest thing you ever saw. (*Chuckling.*)

JOHNSON: (*Chuckling.*) Serve him right.

CHARLIE: Had a month in Monte with a bit I was running round with, then came home and ditched her – and went in with Finkelstein on some very pretty deals. If you're smart, I might let you into something – but – you've got to be smart, y'know.

JOHNSON: (*Boastfully.*) Leave it to me, Charlie ol' boy, Why – only today – or yesterday – some time lately – I was somewhere – in an office – sort of office, anyhow – and things looked difficult – fact is, they were being made to look difficult – deliberately being made to look difficult – but I wouldn't stand for it. Oh, no, no. Cut it out, I said, cut it right out. I want my money and I don't leave here till I get it. Sort of man I am now.

CHARLIE: I can see you're getting smart. By the way, seem to be out of change – d'you mind lending me a fiver?

JOHNSON: (*Grandly.*) Certainly not. (*Hands him notes.*) Better make it a tenner.

CHARLIE: (*Rising.*) Thanks, old boy. Anything I can do for you here?

JOHNSON: (*Whispering.*) Yes. Get me a girl – a nice fresh little piece.

CHARLIE: That's easily fixed. A friend of mine, cleverest woman I know, will attend to that – Madame Vulture. (*CHARLIE grins and nods, then goes. JOHNSON turns round, and there, standing just behind him, is this MADAME VULTURE, a tall thin creature in a black feathered evening dress, with the mask face of a vulture, and with hands that have immensely long sharp blood-red nails, like talons. A horrible figure. JOHNSON stares at her, startled and fascinated.*)

MADAME VULTURE: (*With a ghastly playfulness.*) Now I know what you gentlemen are. You won't have this, and you will have that. No use my trying to suit you unless I know what it is you fancy. Big, medium, little? Brunette, redhead, blonde? Experienced or very young? White, I suppose?

JOHNSON: Certainly. Must be white.

MADAM VULTURE: (*A good saleswoman.*) I think you're wise, though, of course, some gentlemen have exotic tastes. White, then. And blonde perhaps? Why not try a nice blonde?

JOHNSON: A nice li'l' blonde would just suit me.

MADAME VULTURE: Or – of course – a pretty little
   brunette?

JOHNSON: Certainly. Just right.

MADAME VULTURE: Not too big, not too old, not too
   experienced, eh?

JOHNSON: (*Coarsely.*) You've got the idea.

MADAME VULTURE: Well, now, I have the very thing for
   you. Absolutely delightful, and quite fresh. Only just
   come into my hands.
   (*These hands are very close to his face.*)

JOHNSON: (*Staring at them.*) I don't like your hands.

MADAME VULTURE: (*With sinister playfulness.*) Now,
   now, Mr Johnson, don't be naughty.

JOHNSON: (*With drunken idiocy.*) I'm very naughty – fella.

MADAME VULTURE: I can see you are. Now then, what
   do you say to this nice fresh little girl?

JOHNSON: Let's have a look at her.

MADAME VULTURE: You understand, my clients are all
   gentlemen of means – I don't believe in a cheap trade –
   so –

JOHNSON: (*Giving her some notes.*) Oh – you won't find me
   mean – so long as you deliver the goods all right.

MADAME VULTURE: The goods, you will see, Mr
   Johnson, will be absolutely charming, just what you
   want.
   (*She goes. JOHNSON takes another drink, giggles a little,
   and the dancing begins again. Then suddenly the music stops,
   everybody is still, and all the lights fade out except a single
   white light on JOHNSON. It is as if time were held up, and
   JOHNSON now spoke from a deeper self.*)

JOHNSON: (*In slow, deep tone.*) Here I sit waiting – a fool. I
   know I am a fool, yet I know too I am no fool. All this
   has always been folly before, but now perhaps, just for
   once, the miracle may happen… They say I am half-
   animal, half-god… Yet I do not think it is entirely the
   animal in me that is waiting here, for the animal must be
   a simple creature, with a few sharp needs, easily
   satisfied… But this is not simple, this lighted and scented
   jungle, where everything has been so carefully devised to

taste bitter-sweet, half-rotten… Even if the animal in me is fed and tickled, it is to arouse the god, grumbling in his sleep… I make a beast of myself, but the beast is no simple animal, though it may have a shaggy hide and claws… It has the god's head, like the Sphinx, which perhaps looks calm because once, ages ago, in a night as big as our centuries, it slaked all its passion… And even here and now, as I sit slavering, sweating and lustful as a cow-led bull, I know that I wish for peace… Let a miracle be worked for me-the-beast, so that the beast shall be satisfied and I shall have peace…without regret, without regret…

(*The lights come up again. The dancing continues. He is his giggling drunken self again. The HEADWAITER now comes to him. But now the HEADWAITER wears a mask, half-human, half-like a toad. And all the guests and waiters are now seen to be grotesquely masked.*)

HEADWAITER: Everything all right, sir?

JOHNSON: (*Drunkenly, staring.*) Who are you?

HEADWAITER: Maitre d'hotel, sir.

JOHNSON: (*Solemnly.*) But you've got a face like a toad.

HEADWAITER: That's right, sir. Toad is the name.

JOHNSON: (*Vaguely, but grandly.*) Well – treat me all right – and I'll be all right with you. When I've had few more drinks and got nice li'l' girl, life'll be fine, fine. I can feel it bubbling up – fine, fine stuff. Sitting on top o' the world, I am. An' that's where you've got to sit, right on top of it.

(*The floor has now been cleared, as if for a floor show, and in a hard bright light and to fast loud music four tap dancers, two young men in evening clothes and top hats, and two girls, almost naked but wearing coloured top hats, do a fast tap routine. When they have done, there is some applause from the masked guests sitting round, and JOHNSON joins in with enthusiasm. There is a roll on the drum, and there appears on the little platform at the back, where there is a microphone, the COMPERE of the floor show, who is in evening dress, but also wears the mortar board and the MA gown of the unpleasant SCHOOLMASTER whom we saw in the office. The truth is that he is both the COMPERE of the floor show and that unpleasant SCHOOLMASTER, one of those telescoped personalities we often meet in dreams.*)

COMPERE-SCHOOLMASTER: (*At microphone.*) And now, friends, before commencing our floor show, in which I can promise you a big surprise, I want you to give a hand to the boy who's been stealing the front pages and winning all hearts lately – the new champ – Jim Gorilla! (*A powerful fellow in evening dress, wearing a huge grinning monkey-mask, comes forward, holding his hands together above his head in the manner of a boxer saluting his audience. He is loudly applauded, JOHNSON being prominent among the applauders. GORILLA shakes hands with JOHNSON, who is still sitting at his table. Then one of PORKER's girls – it might be DOT or it might be MAISIE; who knows? – rushes forward to embrace GORILLA, who carries her off to his table.*)

(*At microphone.*) And now, friends, a new novelty act, the first time here, and I know it will be a socko number. Robert Johnson – who will make an exhibition of himself. Give him a hand, friends.

JOHNSON: (*Staggering up, surprised.*) Wha' – me?

COMPERE-SCHOOLMASTER: (*At microphone, pointing.*) Robert Johnson! (*JOHNSON is now in the centre of the floor, with the lights on him, and the other guests all sitting round waiting. We hear the soft jigging music suitable for a clown routine.*)

JOHNSON: (*Drunkenly.*) I dunno wha's the idea – but you're all very nice people – I'm a nice fella too – and so le's all be jolly – wha' about a drink? (*They laugh at him. And now a waiter wearing a clown's mask brings on a small table, chair, and large trick bottle of champagne. He puts down the table, offers the chair to JOHNSON, then pulls it away so that JOHNSON falls heavily, protesting amidst laughter. When JOHNSON is finally seated, there is comic business with the trick champagne. WAITER pretends to rub it in JOHNSON's hair, and so forth. Finally, when WAITER goes, JOHNSON is sitting on the floor, very silly, singing and giggling, while the other guests laugh at him. There should be more and more cruelty in their laughter.*)

(*In maudlin style.*) Y'know, funny thing about me is – they think I'm nice respec'able man – they do, honestly. Responsible position in old firm. Wife, son, daughter. All very, very respec'able. 'Morning, Mr Shonson, 'Morning, Mr Shonson. 'Evening, Shonson. How are you today? Anything further, Mr Shonson? All like that, see? Jus' rubbish. All the time jus' a clown, tha's me – a clown. A *nice* clown, mark you – oh, yes – a *nice*, nice clown – (*Giggles.*)

(*The other guests throw rolls of bread at him, one idiotic youth coming very close and throwing his roll very savagely. JOHNSON does not like this, and scrambles to his feet, rather suspicious but filled with self-pity.*)

Steady – steady – don' be too rough with poor ol' Shonson – poor ol' boy! Where's nice li'l' girl they promised me, eh?

GORILLA: (*At back.*) Oh, she'll be along.

JOHNSON: (*Singing drunkenly.*) We're going to have good ti-ime. We're all going to have good ti-ime.

CHARLIE: (*From back, calling loudly.*) Got any money, Johnson old boy?

JOHNSON: (*With drunken dignity.*) Certainly, certainly got money. Want shome? (*Flings up handful of notes.*) Take it, take it, take it. Nothing to me. I'm Robert Johnson. Take it all.

(*He flings up several handfuls of notes and now there is a scrimmage round him of the male guests, all fighting to pick up the notes. JOHNSON, muttering about the little girl they promised him, pushes his way out, and as soon as he does all the lights on this dance floor rapidly fade. Meanwhile, curtains have been drawn to reveal a little private room, almost entirely filled by a divan. It should be flooded with coloured light – light purple or deep pink. We see JOHNSON sitting on this divan, and now CHARLIE comes into this little room, wearing a wolf's mask.*)

CHARLIE: Now then, old boy, see you've found the right place.

JOHNSON: (*Surprised and suspicious.*) You – Charlie?

CHARLIE: Sure – your old pal.

73

JOHNSON: You're looking dam' queer now, Charlie.
Where's the li'l' girl you promised me?

CHARLIE: Here she is.

(*He steps back and MADAME VULTURE comes in, bringing
with her a young GIRL in a simple (preferably white) evening
dress and wearing a domino mask of the same material.*)

MADAME VULTURE: Here she is, just what you wanted.
(*To the GIRL, as she shrinks.*) Don't be a fool. Have a good
time.

(*She laughs and CHARLIE laughs in a wolf-like manner
and they go. JOHNSON tries to pull the GIRL nearer to
him, but she shrinks away. This goes on throughout his dialogue
that follows. The GIRL always resists but with the minimum
of effort, shrinking and slightly pulling herself away from
him rather than actively resisting him. Beginning the whole
scene in a sullen, suspicious, bestial mood, he rapidly gets
worse as it develops.*)

JOHNSON: And a very nice li'l' piece too. *Very* nice. Don't
be silly. Nobody's going to hurt you. Jus' going to have a
good time. (*As she resists again, angrily.*) Wha's the idea,
eh? Who d'you think you are, anyhow? Lemme tell you,
you're jus' a li'l' bit, tha's all, jus' a tuppenny-ha'penny
li'l' bit o' fluff. Bought an' paid for too, don' forget that.
An' don' think I'm not good enough for you, because
lemme tell you I am. Man of the world, I am. Worth a
dozen o' the sort o' young sprigs you like. Come here.
I'm here to have a good time and I've paid for it and I'll
see I get it. And if you won't be a sport and join in, I'll
damn well make you, see? Let's have a look at you. First
thing, we'll have that silly mask off. Come on, take it off.
(*She shakes her head, succeeds in turning away again and
evading his efforts to remove the mask himself, but now we
can hear her crying. This makes him angrier.*)
Oh – for God's sake – don't start crying. What good are
you, anyway? Come on, come on, you miserable little
sniffler – if you think I'm going to be soft with you, let
you get away with that stuff, you're all wrong. I know all
the tricks, don't forget. Come on.
(*Now he has seized her very roughly, but at this moment a
YOUTH, wearing an ordinary lounge suit, but masked like
the girl, dashes into the scene.*)

YOUTH: Leave her alone.

JOHNSON: (*Very angrily.*) Now don't *you* start interfering, whoever you are, because I won't stand for it. Clear out. (*He leaves the GIRL to threaten the YOUTH, which gives the GIRL a chance to slip past him, and the YOUTH hurries out of this little room on to the dance floor, which is now half-lit and is seen to be deserted.*)

JOHNSON: (*Mad with rage, coming out of little room.*) Oh – no – you don't. You two aren't going to make a monkey out of me. Damn you, get out! (*He pulls the GIRL out of the YOUTH's grasp and flings her to one side, then after a short struggle with the YOUTH, JOHNSON picks up a knife from the nearest table and in a blind fury, grunting, he repeatedly stabs the YOUTH, who sinks, moaning. JOHNSON, exhausted, panting, leans against the nearest table. The GIRL gives a scream and hurries across to the YOUTH, raising his head from the floor. Neither is wearing a mask now, and we recognise them as FREDA and RICHARD.*)

FREDA: (*In anguish.*) Richard, Richard! (*JOHNSON turns and bends down and looks with horror into the two faces, then comes staggering down.*)

JOHNSON: (*Whispering in horror.*) Freda! Richard! Oh God! – I didn't know. I didn't know. (*All the night club people, guests and waiters, all masked, now come crowding down, moving slowly in a dense mass, hiding FREDA and RICHARD. They all make a strange hissing sound.*) (*Still whispering.*) Oh God! What did I do?

A VOICE FROM THE CROWD: (*Frightened.*) He's coming, he's coming. (*The crowd now changes its hissing to a queer low moaning and they all point forward, while slowly retreating. JOHNSON notices this.*)

JOHNSON: (*In dull, hopeless tone.*) Something terrible comes…terrible to them, but no longer terrible to me, because now I am already in Hell… There cannot be a deeper Hell than this… I see now that Hell is only a place where you can still think and remember… I am not afraid… I can even hope, for perhaps I only wait my

turn to be blotted out, a thing badly made at last thrown
on the dust heap…

(*The crowd has vanished now. There is no light anywhere but
on JOHNSON himself, who is looking towards us. Now the
music, which has been keeping up a thin high tremulo, flares
into heavy menacing brass, with the theme we heard at the
end of Act One. A tall, majestic, cloaked FIGURE now appears,
walking into the scene from our side of it. As soon as he is
near JOHNSON, he turns and we see again the terrible
shining death's head. There is a pause.*)

If you are Death, I hope you are his very self, final,
omnipotent, extinguishing for ever the last glimmer of
memory… If you are that Death, I am not afraid… I
welcome you… Come, blot me out for good and all…
that is all I am fit for, to be destroyed.

THE FIGURE: (*In deep mocking tone.*) And what of the
thudding of the clay on the coffin, the white maggots and
the worms?

JOHNSON: Now that I still live but am in Hell, they are a
kind of peace. The world will be cleaner when my brain
has rotted and the worms have eaten me to the bone. (*A
pause, then loudly, angrily.*) Well – have you no force in
your arm or even no quick poison in your breath?

THE FIGURE: (*Removing mask, calmly.*) I said you were a
fool, Robert.

JOHNSON: (*Staring.*) You again.

THE FIGURE: (*Rather amused.*) A fool, I said, Robert.

JOHNSON: (*Tragically.*) You do not know me. I am worse
than a fool now.

THE FIGURE: (*Coolly.*) No, no. Don't flatter yourself.

JOHNSON: (*Distressed.*) Didn't you see? My own daughter –
my son – were here – and I – and I – oh! horrible,
horrible!

THE FIGURE: (*Going over to him.*) There are no human
instruments created solely for our satisfaction, Robert.
There are only persons. They are all sons and daughters,
you see.

JOHNSON: I see that – and a thousand other things – now.
But too late! My own children –

THE FIGURE: (*Sharply.*) No, no. Masks and shadows and dreams!

JOHNSON: (*Vehemently.*) They came here, I tell you, and I didn't know them – and I –

THE FIGURE: (*With authority.*) They never came here. Listen!

RICHARD: (*Off, voice exactly as in last scene.*) I thought I'd tell him it was all right and I was sorry and all that, but it was too late then – he couldn't understand what anybody was saying to him.

FREDA: (*Off, voice as before.*) Perhaps if you thought it, he got it somehow. You know, I used to think of him as being quite old –

RICHARD: (*Off, as before.*) Lord yes! – so did I. Terribly old.

FREDA: (*Off, as before.*) I know. Well, just lately I've suddenly seen he isn't really old – I mean – he wasn't…

JOHNSON: Thank God for His mercy! If they were only shadows, that is no merit of mine. What I did, I did.

THE FIGURE: No, for these shadows were of your own making, and it was yourself reproaching yourself. Listen!

CLERGYMAN: (*Off.*) If after the manner of men I have fought with beasts at Ephesus, what advantageth it me, if the dead rise not? Let us eat and drink, for tomorrow we die. Be not deceived: evil communications corrupt good manners…

JOHNSON: (*Alarmed.*) A funeral service?

THE FIGURE: Yours.

JOHNSON: They think I'm dead?

THE FIGURE: Yes.

JOHNSON: (*Agitated.*) And there they are – Jill, Freda, Richard – unhappy. And I'm here. Oh – horrible! What a swine I am!

THE FIGURE: (*Cheerfully, but gently.*) No, no. A fool perhaps, an average sort of fool. (*Pauses, considering him.*) Robert, I think you'd better go on to the Inn now.

JOHNSON: (*Sharply.*) I want to go back to my home, to tell them I'm not really dead – to try and comfort them.

THE FIGURE: (*With great authority.*) You can't go back. In that world you *are* really dead. To try and force your way

77

back there would be to bring evil into your own house. You must take your road. But you can stay a little while at the Inn first.

JOHNSON: What inn is this?

THE FIGURE: Call it, if you like, the Inn at the End of the World. They are expecting you there,

JOHNSON: I have no money now. I flung it all away.

THE FIGURE: You will not need any.

JOHNSON: What shall I find there?

THE FIGURE: I do not know what things have illuminated your mind and touched your heart.

JOHNSON: But how do I go there?

THE FIGURE: That way will do.

(*He points, and JOHNSON turns. The small door behind him is now slowly opening and through it is flooding a golden light, very bright on the darkened stage. Very faintly we hear an exquisite strain of music.*)

And I hope you will be happy there.

JOHNSON: (*Sadly.*) I don't deserve to be happy.

FIGURE: (*In a ringing tone.*) Then I think you may be.

As JOHNSON moves slowly towards the open door and the light and the music swells up, down comes the curtain and the Act is at an end.

ACT THREE

*Once again we see the hall of JOHNSON's house, but now it is early
evening, two days after the funeral, and the house looks much warmer
and more cheerful than it did before. Through the door from the
drawing-room come MR CLAYTON and RICHARD. They go to the
stand for MR CLAYTON's hat and coat.*

RICHARD: It was awfully good of you to come along, Mr
　　Clayton.

CLAYTON: No, no. Least I could do – help to get things
　　straightened out for you. (*Pauses, regarding him.*) You're
　　uncommonly like your father, y'know.

RICHARD: (*Pleased.*) That's what a lot of people say.

CLAYTON: Yes, you remind me of him as he was when he
　　first came to us as a junior clerk – though he'd be
　　younger then than you are now.

RICHARD: Yes, he was.

CLAYTON: (*A reminiscent old gentleman.*) A bit careless at
　　first, of course, like all youngsters, but a wonderfully
　　steady and dependable fellow once he'd settled down. I
　　was just remembering, in there, the time when I first
　　promoted him to his own desk. We used to make a little
　　ceremony of it in those days in the City – glass of wine
　　together, that sort of thing.
　　(*GEORGE NOBLE and FREDA now come out of the
　　drawing-room, and CLAYTON, ready to go, looks across at
　　NOBLE.*)
　　I don't think you go my way, Mr Noble, do you?

NOBLE: No, 'fraid I don't.

CLAYTON: Well, I'll be going. (*Shaking hands with NOBLE
　　and FREDA.*) And my best respects to your mother,
　　young lady. Good night.

NOBLE/FREDA: Good night.
　　(*RICHARD goes out with CLAYTON, while NOBLE and
　　FREDA go to the stand for NOBLE's hat and coat, and
　　NOBLE continues a conversation obviously begun in the
　　drawing-room.*)

NOBLE: Yes, he was a fine chap all right, Robert was. Always said so, ever since we stopped fighting when we were kids. He did me many a good turn.

FREDA: I'm glad.

NOBLE: (*Suddenly remembering with humorous emphasis.*) Mind you, Freda, I once did him a *tremendous* good turn. In fact, if I hadn't, you wouldn't be here.

FREDA: (*Amused.*) Why? What do you mean?

NOBLE: (*Chuckling.*) It was I who first introduced your father to your mother. At a dance – oh – must be nearly thirty years ago. I was thinking about it when we were talking in there. Funny how these things suddenly come back. I could almost remember the very tunes they played that night. (*They move.*)

FREDA: (*Going.*) I wish you'd tell me sometime, Uncle George.

NOBLE: (*Going.*) Tell you what, Freda?

FREDA: (*Smilingly, as they are at door.*) Tell me what were the tunes they played that night at the dance.

(*They have gone out, and now, from the opposite side, JILL enters slowly, stopping before she arrives in the centre. She is still in black, of course, but she is no longer the wan figure we saw before. FREDA and RICHARD, talking quietly, come in from the other side. FREDA suddenly sees her mother standing there.*)

(*Happily surprised.*) Why – mother – you look different.

JILL: (*Smiling, holding out a hand.*) I know, darling – and I feel different.

(*They go over to her.*)

You see, I know. I suddenly saw – quite clearly – everything's all right – really all right – *now*…

(*And as she smiles at her children, the light fades quickly, the scene goes, as we hear music again, first rather sombre but then quickening to a delicious little tune… We still hear the tune softly as we look at the Inn, which seems – as we shall soon hear it is – a rum place. At one side a large staircase comes down, almost at right angles to our line of sight, and underneath this staircase, where it makes a little wall, facing us, is a kind of cosy corner, with a small dining-table and some chairs, some bookshelves let into the wall, a curtained*) *window, and a few framed photographs and small oldish pictures. On the other side is a large window, through which light is streaming. Farther back there does not seem to be anything very much – we merely have a vague impression of a high curtain making a shadowy back wall. JOHNSON enters, wearing a thick travelling overcoat and underneath that a country suit. He is just removing his bowler hat. Behind him there enters the inn PORTER, a stalwart, pleasant-faced fellow, who is carrying JOHNSON's small bag. JOHNSON looks about him, still bewildered but now quite pleasantly bewildered.)*

PORTER: Now, sir, I'll put your bag and coat where I can lay hands on 'em the minute they're wanted.

JOHNSON: (*Handing over his hat and coat.*) Good.

PORTER: (*Who has taken the coat.*) Nice thick coat too, sir – and you're quite right, for it gets cold here late at night. High up, you see, that's what we are – high up, Mr Johnson.

JOHNSON: (*Surprised.*) How do you know my name?

PORTER: (*Smiling.*) Oh – we were expecting you.

JOHNSON: But I don't see how you could have been expecting me.

PORTER: (*Who is perhaps more artful than he looks.*) Why, sir, don't you like being expected?

JOHNSON: Well – yes – I suppose we all do.

PORTER: (*As if that settles it.*) Well, there you are, sir. (*JOHNSON gives him a puzzled glance, then moves down a pace or two, looking about him. Then he sees that the PORTER is still waiting, as if for a tip, and so feels in his pockets.*)

JOHNSON: Oh – er – sorry. I don't seem to have any money with me.

PORTER: (*Coming forward again.*) That's all right, sir. Don't take money here. No use for it. But – there's other and better ways of saying 'Thank you', y'know, sir.

JOHNSON: (*Staring at him.*) I don't understand you. (*Then, with sudden recognition.*) Here, but wait a minute I know you.

PORTER: (*Pleased.*) Ah – now then, you're talking, sir. And that's what we like here. No money – but just what you did now, sir – letting your face light up.

JOHNSON: (*Triumphantly.*) I know – I know!

PORTER: (*Chuckling.*) Are you sure, sir?

JOHNSON: (*Triumphantly.*) Yes, of course, I am. You're Jim Kirkland.

PORTER: Right, sir! Dead right!

JOHNSON: (*All happy reminiscence.*) Why, Jim, you were one of my great heroes. Good Lord! – I remember my father taking me to the Lancashire match for a birthday treat – I must have been about twelve – and I saw you make a hundred and seventy-eight not out. What an innings! Comes back to me now, clear as crystal. A smoking hot morning in July. I can smell the tar on the streets. I can taste the ginger beer I had. I can still see your bat flashing in the sun. What a day! Jim Kirkland – (*He shakes hands with boyish enthusiasm.*)
This is a great moment for me.

PORTER: Proud and happy, sir, proud and happy!

JOHNSON: There's a poem about old cricketers, Jim. Did you ever read it? How did it end? 'As the run-stealers flicker to and fro, to and fro – Oh – my Hornby and my Barlow long ago.'

PORTER: That's it, sir. Well - (*As if about to go.*)

JOHNSON: But what are *you* doing here?

PORTER: (*Smiling.*) Why, sir, meeting you. (*Confidentially.*) It's a rum place, this, you'll see.

JOHNSON: (*Dropping his voice a little.*) I know. That window. Already, outside, it keeps changing.
(*He looks towards the corner under the staircase, and as soon as he does this, a warm light illuminates this corner and the little pictures and photographs seem to glow.*)
And I'm sure some of these pictures and photographs…
(*Goes to examine them.*) Why, that's the photograph we had taken at school. I haven't seen it for over thirty years.
(*Sees others.*) And this used to be in my bedroom at home. It's the very same one. And that. No – this wasn't at home – it was at my grandfather's – I used to stare at it for hours – Good Lord! – I know them all, every one. That one I bought myself, first I ever bought – cost me twelve-and-six at a little second-hand shop. You're right, Jim – (*He turns round.*) – This *is* a –

(*But the PORTER has gone. JOHNSON is bewildered. We hear, very faintly, the children's prayer theme from Humperdinck's opera. JOHNSON sits down, and now a woman's voice is heard, as if reading to a child.*)

WOMAN'S VOICE: Near a great forest there lived a poor woodcutter with his wife and his two children. The boy was called Hansel and the girl Gretel. The woodcutter was very poor indeed, and once when there was a famine in that land he could no longer give his wife and children their daily bread...

JOHNSON: (*Sharply, unconsciously.*) Mother!

(*But the voice has stopped. A little waiter has appeared, an oldish chap with white hair and a droll withered-apple face, and as soon as we have a good look at him we can see the old clown look he has. He has one of those rusty Cockney voices so many of the old comedians had, and his name is ALBERT GOOP.*)

ALBERT: Mr Johnson, isn't it, sir?

JOHNSON: Yes.

ALBERT: (*Smiling.*) You'll find everything ready, sir, when you are. The lady was in early, telling me what you liked.

JOHNSON: (*Surprised.*) The lady?

ALBERT: Yes, sir, *your* lady. (*Now, with deliberate comical air.*) So you'll find everything in good trim, I say you'll find everything in good trim.

JOHNSON: (*Staring at him.*) I say – now – wait a minute –

ALBERT: (*Who can't wait.*) Yes, sir. Albert Goop. In the pantomimes at the old Theatre Royal.

JOHNSON: (*Triumphantly.*) Of course!

ALBERT: (*Almost doing his old act now.*) Right, sir. And don't forget the little cane. (*Produces one.*) I say don't forget the little cane.

JOHNSON: You used to be the Baron in *Cinderella* and the captain of the ship in *Robinson Crusoe*, and you always had your little cane, and said things twice. I used to spend hours and hours imitating you when I was a kid. Why, we all worshipped you, Albert Goop!

ALBERT: (*Completely the comedian now, doing steps and everything.*) Every Christmas at the old Theatre Royal,

Longfield, there was Albert with his cane and a big red nose. I say there was Albert with his cane and a big red nose. Ah – happy days, sir, happy days.

JOHNSON: Lord! – I'd count the weeks to those pantomimes – and the next sight of you, Albert.

ALBERT: (*Doing a droll step.*) Thank you very much. (*And now JOHNSON says it with him and does the step too.*) I say thank you very much.

(*JOHNSON laughs, then stares in astonishment out of the window, finally grinning like a schoolboy.*)

JOHNSON: Albert – I distinctly saw a stage coach go down that road – and I'll swear Mr Pickwick was on it, with Sam Weller – and – I think – fat old Mr Weller was driving. What do you think about that, Albert?

ALBERT: Doesn't surprise me. I say it doesn't surprise me. You can see anything through that window. I once saw 'alf the bill at the old Middlesex through it – Dan Leno, R G Knowles, Lottie Collins, everybody – then – gone like a puff o' smoke – I say gone like a puff o' smoke.

JOHNSON: By jove, Albert – you know, Jim Kirkland's right. It's a rum place, this.

ALBERT: Rum! It's the rummest you ever saw, this is. Why, it hasn't started on you yet. You wait – I say you wait.

JOHNSON: Wait for what, Albert?

ALBERT: Now don't ask questions, sir. Just let things happen. That's the way to go on here, sir – just let things happen.

JOHNSON: Then I'll wait for the lady, Albert.

ALBERT: She'll appreciate it, sir. I say she'll appreciate it. (*They are now standing together near the foot of the stairs, and from farther up the stairs we hear the sound of a boy's voice. They both look up.*)

TOM: (*Off.*) Well, where is he then? I want to talk to him.

JOHNSON: (*Startled.*) Why, that's Tom's voice.

ALBERT: Your brother, sir?

JOHNSON: Yes, but he was killed in the War –

ALBERT: (*Baffled.*) War? What war?

(*TOM comes running down the stairs. He is a fine-looking lad in his middle teens, dressed in the style of thirty-five years ago.*)

TOM: Bob, you chump! Now then, Albert, buzz off – this is private.
(*ALBERT goes.*)
Just like you, Bob, to be so slow. You ought to have known this is the place to be in. Always keep me waiting, you old fat-head

JOHNSON: (*Slowly, rather painfully.*) Sorry, Tom. I didn't – well, I suppose I didn't know the way –

TOM: (*Indicating the window.*) Look there!

JOHNSON: (*Staring.*) Why – it's exactly what we used to see from our bedroom at that farm we stayed at those three summers. Look – the two haystacks – the road dipping down – the pond we had the raft on – that old cart –

TOM: The one you fell off, you ass.

JOHNSON: (*A boy again.*) Well, don't forget you fell in the pond.
(*As he looks again, we hear the music that JOHNSON listened to in the office, and now the girl's voice comes in again, high and trailing. JOHNSON listens – then speaks very quietly.*)
I've heard that before, in the strangest places, and it never lasts long. But at least it seems to belong here, and it never did anywhere before.

TOM: What are you talking about?

JOHNSON: Didn't you hear it?

TOM: I didn't hear anything. Oh – Lord! – look who's here.
(*MORRISON, a pleasant looking, middle-aged schoolmaster, wearing an old blazer and smoking a pipe, has just entered, in the corner by the staircase, and now the warm light comes on there.*)

JOHNSON: (*Turning.*) Mr Morrison!

MORRISON: (*Coolly.*) Hello! Both Johnsons at once.

TOM: Yes, sir, but I'm pushing off. See you later, Bob.

JOHNSON: (*With sudden urgency.*) Tom!

TOM: (*Cheerfully, in a hurry, going upstairs.*) All right, chump, I'll see you later. I want to talk to old funny-face upstairs about some bait he promised me.

JOHNSON: (*Going to foot of stairs and calling, distressed.*) Tom! Tom!

MORRISON: (*As JOHNSON slowly comes nearer.*) Tom's had enough of my company. I'm afraid he doesn't like schoolmasters, even out of hours. (*Pauses, then noting JOHNSON's distress.*) Hello, what's worrying you, Robert?

JOHNSON: (*With an effort.*) It was – only seeing Tom again – after so long a time –

MORRISON: Ah – there's none of that time here, y'know. You must have brought a bit of it with you. Odd place this, Robert. Noticed the books?

JOHNSON: (*In boyish tones.*) No, sir.

MORRISON: (*Smiling.*) And I imagined I'd taught you to appreciate good literature. Have a look.

JOHNSON: (*Going up to the books.*) Why, they're all my old ones. Here's my old copy of *Don Quixote.* (*Turns the pages.*) With all the pictures. I remember the first time I read this. It was one Christmas, a real snowy Christmas, and I'd had to go to bed with a snivelling cold – and I remember curling up in bed, very cosy, with the snow thickening on the window panes and the cold blue daylight dying – and first staring at the pictures – (*As he stands there, saying this, with the book in his hand, the light in that corner fades rapidly, and a bright moonlight streams through the window opposite, and we hear a lance tapping at the sill. The next moment, DON QUIXOTE, wearing old armour but no head-piece, is standing there, his white hair and beard and long lined fantastic face very sharply defined by the light, which also catches JOHNSON's face in a moment or two, when he steps forward.*)

DON QUIXOTE: (*Gravely.*) Your pardon, sirs, but this night should bring me to one of the most famous adventures that ever was seen, for this whole region abounds with wicked enchanters and there are great wrongs to be redressed...

JOHNSON: (*Stepping forward, eagerly.*) Yes, just the same. Don Quixote, you don't know me, but I remember you.

DON QUIXOTE: I seem to remember a boy in an upstairs room of a small house, far away, one winter's night –

JOHNSON: (*Eagerly.*) Yes, I was that boy. But I didn't think you'd remember.

DON QUIXOTE: (*With a noble breadth.*) Sir, your imagination, your memory of us, your affection for us, these are our life – all that we have.

JOHNSON: Yes, I think I understand that.

DON QUIXOTE: Your great poet once said that the best of our kind are but shadows, though I think he knew that your kind too – who appear so solid to yourselves for a little time – are also only shadows. And perhaps you too take life from the mind that beholds you and your little tale, so that you live as we must do, in another and greater being's imagination, memory and affection. (*Pause.*) Do you notice any change in me?

JOHNSON: (*Gently, hesitantly.*) Only – perhaps – you seem a trifle older –

DON QUIXOTE: (*Sadly.*) Yes. You see, we are being forgotten. We are shadows even to shadows, and play in a dream within a dream.

JOHNSON: (*With feeling.*) I am glad to have seen you again, Don Quixote.

DON QUIXOTE: (*In new and ringing tone.*) Sir, I take life from your remembrance. If you should see my squire, Sancho Panza, tell him to follow me instantly along the highroad. Farewell, good sirs.

(*He salutes then and disappears. The bright moonlight goes with him, and now JOHNSON is back in the lighted corner, looking at the books again.*)

JOHNSON: Yes, yes. They're all my old ones. *Grimm's Fairy Tales, The Arabian Nights* I used to crayon. The Shakespeare I had at school with you.

(*As he stands there, with MORRISON, looking at the books, we hear voices, masculine and feminine, not coming from any one place, speaking famous lines.*)

A VOICE: Daffodils,
That come before the swallow dares and take
The winds of March with beauty…

A VOICE: Will no one tell me what she sings?
Perhaps the plaintive numbers flow
For old, unhappy, far-off things
And battles long ago…

A VOICE: The long day wanes: the slow moon climbs; the deep

    Moans round with many voices. Come, my friends,

    'Tis not too late to seek a newer world…

A VOICE: I cannot praise a fugitive and cloister'd virtue, unexercised and unbreath'd, that never sallies out and sees her adversary…

A VOICE: Or ever the silver cord be loosed, or the golden bowl be broken…

    Men must endure

    Their going hence, even as their coming hither:

    Ripeness is all…

A VOICE: The Lord is my Shepherd; I shall not want…

JOHNSON: (*Sitting, slowly and regretfully.*) Ever since I saw you last, these many years, I think I have been foolish and ignorant, for you taught me long ago that in these voices, which come so quickly when we call on them, I would find wisdom and beauty. Though I remembered this, and sometimes, when business was not pressing and pleasure began to pall, I heard echoes of the voices again, I did not ask them to give me their treasure. But always I felt there was a time ahead when at last I could sit by the fire and listen to them again; and now it seems there is no such time for me, only this brief last hour…

MORRISON: It doesn't matter, Robert. We don't know what Time is, let alone how it shall be divided for us. And this isn't the last frontier of Beauty. (*In brisker tone.*) I'm glad to have seen you again, Robert.

JOHNSON: (*A boy again, shyly.*) And I you, sir. I always liked you the best, y'know, sir.

MORRISON: (*Smiling.*) If you hadn't I shouldn't have been here. Well – I must go.

    (*As MORRISON goes, a BARMAN in a striped jacket comes round the corner of the staircase into the little scene, carrying a tray with two wine glasses on it. This BARMAN approaches JOHNSON as the latter watches MORRISON go.*)

BARMAN: Here you are, Mr Johnson. Nice glass o' wine too.

JOHNSON: (*Turning.*) Oh – thanks. Here, I say, I've seen you before somewhere.

BARMAN: Now I'll bet you can't remember, Mr Johnson. I said to Albert when I begged him to let me bring these in and just do something for you, I said: 'I'll bet he won't remember me.'

JOHNSON: A street somewhere…a wet night…

BARMAN: You're getting it, sir, you're getting it. I was down and out, and I'd been along to a place near Cheapside to try and get a caretaker's job, and I hadn't got it and I felt like chucking myself in the river. And I stopped you and asked you if you could spare a copper –

JOHNSON: Yes, I remember now. I'd just had a bit of luck at the office.

BARMAN: You said so, when you gave me that ten bob. And that ten bob made all the difference. It made me feel better, to start with, and then I spent it getting a train up to my sister's, and her husband found me a bit of a job, and so I started all over again. In a few months I was a different chap altogether from the one that stopped you that night. All on account o' that ten bob, Mr Johnson.

JOHNSON: Yes, but how do you know my name?

BARMAN: (*Chuckling.*) Ah – there isn't much we don't know round here, sir. Well, now, Mr Clayton ordered these two glasses of wine.

JOHNSON: (*Surprised.*) Mr Clayton?

BARMAN: That's right, sir. Your boss, isn't he?

JOHNSON: He was.

BARMAN: And your friend too before you'd finished, eh, sir?

JOHNSON: Yes, my friend too.

BARMAN: (*Chuckling.*) Wouldn't be here if he wasn't. And here he is, right on the dot.

(*And so he is, not the CLAYTON we met in the hall, but twenty-five years younger, dressed in business clothes of a pre-War cut. He is in good spirits, all smiling.*)

CLAYTON: Ah – thanks.

(*BARMAN goes. JOHNSON and CLAYTON both take glasses.*)

Well, Johnson, I'm glad you could join me in a glass of wine.

89

JOHNSON: (*Shyly, the junior clerk again.*) It's very good of you, Mr Clayton.

CLAYTON: Not at all. Always our custom here, y'know.

JOHNSON: (*Eagerly, hopefully.*) Sir – you don't mean – ?

CLAYTON: (*Significantly.*) Yes, my dear fellow. (*Raising glass.*) The firm!

JOHNSON: (*Raising his glass.*) The firm!
(*They drink.*)

CLAYTON: (*Sitting down.*) Yes, Johnson, your probationary period is now over. We all feel you've worked very well. We all like you. And now I'm glad to say you may consider yourself definitely one of the London staff of Bolt, Cross and Clayton. And it will be your own fault, not ours, if you aren't with us a long time.

JOHNSON: (*Pleased.*) I hope I am, sir.

CLAYTON: I hope so too. From now on, you'll have your own desk, of course, and the board has decided to raise your salary in accordance with our usual custom – by seventy-five pounds a year.

JOHNSON: (*Delighted.*) Thank you, sir. I'll try to do my best for the firm.

CLAYTON: That's all we ask, Johnson. Let's see – you're not married yet?

JOHNSON: (*Shyly.*) No, Mr Clayton.

CLAYTON: Thinking of it?

JOHNSON: (*Grinning, awkwardly.*) Well – no – I'm not, sir. Haven't met her yet.

CLAYTON: (*Jovially.*) You will, you will. You look to me like a marrying man, Johnson. (*Rising.*) Well, best of luck. I won't keep you. Expect you want to dance.

JOHNSON: (*Puzzled.*) To dance?
(*The lights change, and now the staircase and all the space behind are lit with a greeny-blue light that has something ghostly about it, although it is by no means dim and subdued. The orchestra is softly playing the 'Valse Bleu'. A group of young people, girls and young men, all in pre-War evening clothes, come down the stairs, laughing and flirting, and then go waltzing away. The last to come down is GEORGE NOBLE, now a young sprig in his early twenties, with a glass of claret cup in his hand.*)

CLAYTON: There you are, you see.

(*He goes out, chuckling, and now the warm light in this cosy corner fades out, but where NOBLE is standing near the bottom of the stairs is now strongly lit, and JOHNSON walks into this light. The greeny-blue light has gone. We can only see JOHNSON and NOBLE, but we can still hear, very faintly, the 'Valse Bleu'.*)

NOBLE: (*Excitedly.*) Well, Bob, don't say I never do you a good turn.

JOHNSON: (*Puzzled.*) All right. But why, George?

NOBLE: Don't be an ass. You asked me to find out who she is, and I've found out who she is.

JOHNSON: (*Puzzled.*) Who is she?

(*But now he is suddenly young again, at that dance, waiting to be told who she is.*)

Yes, of course. Sorry, George! Good work, old boy! Well, who is she? Where does she live?

NOBLE: That's better. Now that I've pulled it off, I thought you were goig to have the cheek to pretend it didn't matter and you weren't completely dotty on the girl not half an hour ago.

JOHNSON: (*Eagerly.*) Come on! Who is she?

NOBLE: Her name's Jill Gregg, and her mother's a widow, and they live out at Richmond.

JOHNSON: (*Slowly, wonderingly.*) Jill Gregg – Jill!

NOBLE: *And* I've been introduced, *and* now I can introduce you, so what more do you want?

JOHNSON: (*Eagerly.*) Nothing – except lead me to her.

NOBLE: Yes, if you don't look pretty smart about it, I'll cut you out myself. And even if I don't, there are plenty more who will, especially a hefty chappie with a dragoon's moustache, who's putting in some heavy work with her.

JOHNSON: (*Gaily.*) He won't have a chance. I'll show him.

NOBLE: All right, well get this into your fat head. I'll meet you outside the supper room in about ten minutes, and I'll have her there waiting for you – even if I've to have that bloke with the moustache thrown out. Right?

JOHNSON: (*With enthusiasm.*) George, you're a brick.

NOBLE: I know. Not that I think you'll get anywhere with her. Too much class for you, my boy – you'll see. Still, you can try. Outside the supper room – in ten minutes. (*NOBLE goes waltzing away. JOHNSON steps forward, as the lights begin to fade near the bottom of the staircase and come into the corner where the table and chairs are.*)

JOHNSON: Good old George! (*Slowly, tasting it.*) Jill. Jill Gregg. Jill… Richmond… (*Then exultantly, as if remembering everything.*) Yes, yes. My Jill!
(*Now there enters into the corner a small bearded doctor, dressed in the style of 1914, still putting away the last of his things into his black bag.*)

DOCTOR: (*With mock sternness.*) Mr Johnson!

JOHNSON: (*Coming forward, now an anxious young husband.*) Yes – doctor?

DOCTOR: Didn't I tell you to clear out and stay out for a few hours – to take a walk – or play billiards – or even get drunk – ?

JOHNSON: (*Apologetically.*) I know. But I simply couldn't. I had to come back. (*Almost sweating with anxiety.*) Doctor – is it – is it – going to be all right?

DOCTOR: (*Teasing him.*) As I told you before, why be so suspicious? Your wife's a sound healthy young woman, who's doing what Nature wants her to do.

JOHNSON: (*Gloomily.*) I know. But Nature can want you to do something and then go and let you down when you do it.

DOCTOR: (*Easily.*) Ah – that's where Science has to step in. (*In ordinary conversational style, though really teasing.*) I don't like this business over in Ireland. Officers at the Curragh saying they won't obey their own government. Can't have that, can we? But I've always been a Home Ruler myself. Are you?

JOHNSON: (*Who can't take this stuff in.*) Oh – I dunno –

DOCTOR: (*This is his opportunity.*) Come, come, Mr Johnson! A man in your position ought to take more interest in these things. We fathers – y'know –

JOHNSON: (*Staggered.*) Fathers! Has it – happened?

DOCTOR: Of course it has. A fine boy – nearly eight pounds.

JOHNSON: (*With tremendous excitement.*) Oh – Christmas! – and how's Jill – my wife – ?

DOCTOR: (*Smiling.*) She's all right. Came through it very well. (*Suddenly stern.*) But you can't see her until nurse gives the word. (*At the door.*) Be sensible now!

JOHNSON: (*Enormously relieved and elated.*) Sensible! Sensible be damned! I could pull up oak trees.

(*The DOCTOR has gone now and the light in this corner is fading.*)

Jill's all right. A boy – a fine boy – eight pounds of him. Oh gosh! Just what she wanted. A girl next – yes, must have a girl. A boy – then a girl –

(*As he says this, brilliant sunlight comes flashing through the window, and there, framed in it, are RICHARD and FREDA, gay in holiday clothes and a few years younger, perhaps, than they were in the hall scenes. In high spirits, they call through the open window.*)

RICHARD: Hoy, hoy! Dad!

FREDA: (*Gaily.*) Don't pretend not to know us.

JOHNSON: (*As he turns to look at them.*) Here – wait a minute – (*For at this moment he does not know them.*)

RICHARD: Now, Dad, no funny stuff!

FREDA: (*Excitedly.*) We got right to the top and saw for hundreds of miles, didn't we, Dick?

RICHARD: (*Who thinks he's a realist.*) Well – fifty miles.

FREDA: Oh – much more than that. And some of it was awfully hard going –

RICHARD: (*Grinning.*) She screeched in one place.

FREDA: (*Indignantly.*) That was only because I tore my stocking. You know it was.

RICHARD: Oh well – she wasn't bad, really.

FREDA: And we had a marvellous day, except that you weren't with us. (*Pause.*) What's the matter?

JOHNSON: (*Who has gone closer.*) I'm sorry. I was just thinking – you're a fine pair – just what –

RICHARD: Now, Dad, stop it.

FREDA: Daddy, no teasing.

JOHNSON: (*As it dawns.*) You're my children?

FREDA: Of course we are.

JOHNSON: (*Hastily.*) Yes, yes, of course you must be. Oh –
this is great, isn't it? I'm sorry I was so stupid.

FREDA: Don't you want us?

JOHNSON: Of course I do. I tell you, it's – tremendous.
Come inside, come in at once and talk to me.

RICHARD: No, Dad.

FREDA: We both agreed that wouldn't do, not tonight.

RICHARD: You don't want us here tonight.

JOHNSON: (*Bewildered.*) I don't. How do you know I
don't?

FREDA: We know the pair of you, when you're together,
won't want us.

JOHNSON: The pair of us?

FREDA: (*Enthusiastically.*) Yes. But tomorrow we'll all have
an enormous day. And you're not to be lazy.

RICHARD: (*Also with enthusiasm.*) We'll start just after
breakfast, and climb everything there is.

JOHNSON: (*Dubiously.*) Tomorrow…?

RICHARD: (*Confidently.*) Yes, tomorrow. Don't you believe
in tomorrow?

FREDA: (*Laughingly.*) Tomorrow and tomorrow and
tomorrow – (*She breaks off because she sees something in his
face. Concerned now.*) What's the matter, father?

JOHNSON: (*Slowly.*) Father! How strange that is!
Frightening too!

FREDA: Tell us – please! You don't *tell* us enough.

RICHARD: That's true, Dad. Don't be so grand and so
aloof.

JOHNSON: (*Earnestly.*) You know, I've never felt grand and
aloof. Since you stopped being small children, I've
simply been shy. Sometimes I've even grumbled, not
because I wanted to, but because I couldn't find the sense
and courage to say to you what I wanted to say. Will you
forgive me?

FREDA: But there's nothing to forgive. And we knew how
you felt.

RICHARD: Didn't you with your father?

JOHNSON: (*Slowly.*) Yes, I suppose I did. But there ought
to have been many a word spoken between us – I mean,
between you two and me – when there was only silence

or a stupid show of speech. I think I would have told you more if I'd felt I'd any real wisdom. But I felt I'd so little to give you worth having. For all I knew, you might have already found a wisdom I could never find. You might have stumbled upon the clue that I always missed, the clue to everything, the secret...

FREDA: (*Eagerly, as music plays softly.*) There is a secret, isn't there? Like living in a house where there's a hidden treasure. Oh – Dad – you feel just as I do.

RICHARD: I know. And I believe I've got hold of something.

FREDA: (*Excitedly.*) Richard, you haven't! But don't tell us now. Let's *all* talk about it – tomorrow.

RICHARD: (*Eagerly.*) Right! Tomorrow, eh, Dad?

JOHNSON: (*Slowly, painfully.*) Yes…let's do that… tomorrow. (*He waits a moment, then gently.*) Goodbye, children.

RICHARD: Not goodbye –

FREDA: (*Softly.*) Just – good night, father.
(*And the light is fading rapidly behind them, and they seem to be drifting away.*)

JOHNSON: (*Softly.*) Good night, Richard. Good night, Freda. Good night.
(*They have gone and the window is dark, but now the warm light has come on again in the cosy corner below the staircase, and as JOHNSON stands a moment, ALBERT GOOP comes bustling in, to clear away the wine glasses before laying the table.*)

ALBERT: Everything looking nice and cosy, sir, eh? What do you think of this place?

JOHNSON: (*Sitting down, quietly.*) I recognise it now, Albert.

ALBERT: So you've seen it before, eh?

JOHNSON: Yes, I've caught a glimpse of it many a time, awake and in dreams. But I've never been here long – never long.

ALBERT: (*Chuckling softly.*) Ah – no – that's the trouble, sir.

JOHNSON: (*Very quietly.*) Sometimes I only saw it from a long way off, just the smoke of it rising at the end of a good day. I think sometimes too, when I came nearer and the door opened for me, it all vanished, and I was left bewildered among the great clanking machinery of existence. But it was always here, waiting for me.

ALBERT: That's right, sir. I say that's right. Always waiting for you.

JOHNSON: I know I can't stay here long. I shall have to go soon. And still something – somebody – is missing. This isn't all. There's still an emptiness.

ALBERT: (*Chuckling, as he fusses with the glasses.*) Yes – and why, sir? Because you're beginning to feel a bit lonely. Well, that's all right. I say that's all right. *They* know about that, and so of course they just keep you waiting long enough. Some calls that their artfulness – and so up to a point it is – but I say they know just what's right for a man, see, sir? Look at the very start of it all – Garden of Eden. Was Eve there right at the beginning? No fear. I say no fear! She waits a bit until he's feeling lonely, then up she pops and pretends she's just on time. *They* know. I say *they* know. (*Ready to go now.*) Well, sir, everything's ready when you are. (*As he moves away.*) I say everything's ready when you are, (*Stops, hearing sound upstairs.*) That's her now, sir, you'll see.

(*ALBERT retires, chuckling. JOHNSON goes to the foot of the stairs and looks up. Music begins, softly at first then swelling and surging. A misty light hovering over the staircase now becomes stronger as JILL appears, walking slowly down, looking radiant, dressed in whatever suits her best. JOHNSON stares up at her in wonder and admiration. She stops about two-thirds of the way down, and smiles at him.*)

JILL: Who am I, Robert?

JOHNSON: (*Slowly at first but with mounting excitement.*) You are Jill, my wife. And you are Jill, the mother of my children. And you are Jill, the girl I saw for the first time at a dance nearly thirty years ago. And you are Jill the girl who had not yet been to that dance, who had never seen me, who dreamed perhaps of a lover and a husband very different from me. You are all those, and something more as well, something even more than the Jill who went with me on that wedding journey to Switzerland, so young, so happy. You are the essential Jill, whom I was for ever finding, losing, then finding again. You are my love, the wonder and terror and delight of my heart.

JILL: (*Moving slowly down to him.*) Because at last you say that, I am happy. And like you, I am at peace. How strange it is! We have no more peace in ourselves than you have, but when you find peace in us, then we find it too. Perhaps that is why God created us men and women. (*She turns to the window, through which bright moonlight is streaming.*) Look! What do you see?

JOHNSON: (*Wonderingly, happily.*) The moon begins to rise over the lake again, and the mountains are in deep shadow.

JILL: But already the highest peaks are silver,

JOHNSON: It's the same lake.

JILL: I remember every mountain top.

JOHNSON: We only had a fortnight there.

JILL: (*Hastily.*) Less than that – twelve and a half days.

JOHNSON: (*Happily.*) We sat on the balcony, night after night, and watched that moonrise.

JILL: There was something about that lake – always – that caught at my heart – as you did, Robert.

JOHNSON: I felt then – and tried to say it too, but the words stuck in my throat –

JILL: (*With laughing reproach.*) Too many nice words stuck in that throat of yours, Robert.

JOHNSON: I know. I felt then that for once the world outside ourselves seemed to be the mirror of our hearts. (*To the scene outside.*) Goodbye.

JILL: (*With a touch of alarm.*) Why do you say that?

JOHNSON: (*Gently.*) It seems to me to be fading. Perhaps a mist is coming over it. Sometimes, you remember, there were mists.

(*The moonlight fades out, but as JILL goes closer to him, a warm sunlight begins to stream in, and she turns and sees it.*)

JILL: (*Looking out.*) What do you see now?

JOHNSON: (*Staring.*) Nothing much yet. Wait a minute, though. (*Ecstatically.*) Why, it's the little back garden of the bungalow, the first we ever had.

JILL: (*Quickly.*) I can see my three rose bushes.

JOHNSON: Isn't my old deck-chair still out there?

JILL: Yes, and my gardening basket. I was so proud of that and really I didn't know a thing about gardening then.

JOHNSON: Lord! – I used to sit out there at the weekends as if I were in the middle of a five-hundred-acre estate. And the way I used to trim that privet hedge!

JILL: (*Reproachfully, and suddenly taking the scene from the past into the present.*) Oh! – Robert – you've left all that mess of stuff out there again. Look – that silly big ashtray and pipes and newspapers and that ridiculous old hat –

JOHNSON: (*Impatiently, also turning past into present.*) Well, what does it matter? It's our garden and those are all my things.

JILL: (*Rather sharply now.*) But they look so awful – just as if we didn't care how we looked.

JOHNSON: (*More impatiently.*) But we know we do care how we look – I mean, up to a point – but after all a garden's a place to enjoy yourself in – and –

JILL: (*Cutting in sharply.*) Yes, you've told me that a thousand times already. But it's no reason why a garden should look like a lumber room. And other people see it as well as ourselves – and goodness only knows what Mrs Lee says about it.

JOHNSON: (*Exasperatedly.*) But what the blazes does it matter what Mrs Lee says or thinks about our garden? First, you tell me you can't stand the woman –

JILL: (*Sharply.*) But can't you see that's all the more reason why we shouldn't give her an excuse to criticise us?

JOHNSON: (*Almost shouting now, across that old gulf between the sexes.*) No, I can't see. It all sounds unreasonable and dam' silly to me –

JILL: (*Angrily, betrayed again.*) That's because you're so selfish you look at everything just from your own point of view –

JOHNSON: (*Angrily.*) No, I don't.

JILL: (*Who by this time has been deserted by husband and children, jeered at by all the neighbours, stoned through the streets.*) Yes, you do. You never really *think* about me –

(*But as they stand and glare at each other, the light from the window begins to fade, as if to reproach them. JILL turns, dismayed.*)

Oh – it's going.

JOHNSON: (*Miserably.*) Serves me right! Jill!

JILL: (*Tearful but glad.*) Robert!

(*As they console each other, a rich warm intimate light comes on in the corner where the table is. JILL sees the table and goes over, JOHNSON following her.*)

(*Looking at table and things on it.*) I remember this – you know – so well.

JOHNSON: Do you?

JILL: Yes, don't you?

JOHNSON: (*Considering the table.*) Well, I suppose I would – if I ever remembered such things. Seems all a bit familiar.

JILL: It's all from the third holiday we had after we were married, when Richard was just beginning to walk.

JOHNSON: (*Astonished.*) Can you remember?

JILL: Yes, everything with us in it. Streets, houses, tables, chairs, dishes, knives and forks. All laid out for ever in an enchanted country. Ours.

(*They have now sat down at the table, and ALBERT appears with a tray of magnificent things to eat and a bottle of wine.*)

ALBERT: There you are, sir! Everything that you specially fancy, and all snug and cosy. I say all snug and cosy.

JOHNSON: Yes – grand, Albert!

ALBERT: (*Indicating wine.*) With the landlord's compliments, sir.

JOHNSON: We must drink his health. Jill – the landlord's health!

(*They drink.*)

By the way, who *is* the landlord?

ALBERT: (*Confidentially.*) Couldn't exactly say, sir, and that's a fact, but I've had my suspicions. I say I've had my suspicions.

JOHNSON: What are they?

JILL: (*Rather hastily.*) No, Robert, don't let's bother about him now.

ALBERT: Quite right, ma'am. Besides, there's the message he sent down to be attended to.

JOHNSON: What message? To me?

ALBERT: That's right, sir. He said, 'Ask Mr Johnson what time and place he'd like this to be while he's having his supper.'

JOHNSON: (*Bewildered.*) What time and place?

JILL: Yes, Robert. You can choose. Only don't choose something before I knew you – or I'll be out of it.

JOHNSON: Good Lord – no! (*Thinks a moment.*) Now wait a minute. You know, my cousin George Noble came in and said he'd introduce us, just as he did at that Christmas dance, long ago –

JILL: (*Eagerly.*) When we first met?

JOHNSON: Yes. I thought it was going to happen all over again, but it didn't. Now that's what we'd like, Albert.

ALBERT: (*Going.*) The Christmas dance – ve-ery good, sir.

JOHNSON: (*Calling.*) But – Albert!

ALBERT: (*Halting.*) Sir?

JOHNSON: Could everybody be there, this time?

ALBERT: I'll pass the message on, sir. (*Hurries out.*)

JOHNSON: (*With just the two of them, snug at the table.*) You see, Jill, that was the very beginning for us. And we'll see the beginning again but now we shall know everything that came out of it. We'll be ourselves as we were then but we'll also be all the selves we've been since, so that we'll have *everything.*

JILL: (*Affectionately teasing.*) Aren't you clever?

JOHNSON: Well, you must admit, it's a jolly good idea. Let's see – who gave that dance?

JILL: (*Promptly.*) Some people called Williams.

JOHNSON : You remember everything.

JILL: I'm not likely to forget that. And the funny thing was, as I've told you before, I hardly knew them. And you didn't either, did you?

JOHNSON: No, they were friends of my uncle, George Noble's father. I spotted you the minute we arrived. You were waiting for somebody. I hung about, hoping somebody would introduce us –

JILL: (*Tenderly.*) I know you did. And as a matter of fact I *wasn't* waiting for somebody. No, that's not true – I was. I was waiting for you.

(*As she puts a hand across the table and he takes it, the orchestra slides into the 'Valse Bleu', the lovely greeny-blue, ghostly lights come on, illuminating the whole stage, and all the company come waltzing on from the back. There are the young people we saw before, and others too, and older people, all in the evening clothes of about 1912. In addition there are characters who have previously appeared in this Act, still wearing the same clothes as before, people like TOM, CLAYTON, MORRISON, and even FREDA and RICHARD. Except for the corner where JILL and JOHNSON are sitting, the whole stage is filled with these dancing figures. JOHNSON now turns and looks at them, all happy and excited, like a schoolboy.*)

JOHNSON: (*With mounting excitement.*) Look – there's good old George. It was he who did the trick for us that night. Why, there's Tom…was he there? He might have been, though…and Mr Clayton…he wasn't there, of course… And old Morrison from my school…glorious idea bringing him in… Look, Jill – your mother, having a roaring good time…do you remember how suspicious of me she was at first?… I'll bet Don Quixote's somewhere about… I had a talk to him… And look – Richard – *our* Richard – that's cheek, if you like, coming to dance at the party where his mother met his father!

RICHARD: (*Calling from the crowd of dancers.*) Why don't you two dance?

JOHNSON: (*In high spirits.*) Why not? (*He jumps up and moves forward before turning.*) Come on, Jill – we'll show them.

(*But now when he turns the corner is dark and JILL is no longer there. He is first bewildered, then terribly distressed.*)
Jill! Jill! Where are you? Jill!

(*He is now almost in the centre of the stage, not far from the bottom of the staircase. The dancers are still, and the music has stopped. There is a moment's silence. Then comes the CLERGYMAN's voice from somewhere far away.*)

CLERGYMAN: (*Off.*) Lettest thou thy servant depart in peace according to thy word…

JOHNSON: (*Calling urgently among the deepening shadows.*) Jill! Jill! Where are you? Jill!

(*The sombre theme, announced by heavy brass, that we have heard before, is now heard again. The FIGURE appears, tall, hooded, very impressive, on the staircase. A golden shaft of light, from below, illuminates him, and throws an immense shadow on the high curtain at the back. There is a steely light on JOHNSON's face. The rest are in shadow.*)

THE FIGURE: (*Solemnly.*) Robert Johnson, it is time for you to go.

THE CROWD: (*Drawing back, murmuring.*) The landlord! The landlord!

THE FIGURE: Robert Johnson, you cannot stay here any longer.

JOHNSON: (*Urgently.*) My wife was with me a moment ago. Now she's disappeared. I've lost her. And I must speak to her again.

THE FIGURE: There is no need.

JOHNSON: (*Very urgently.*) Yes, I must.

THE FIGURE: Listen!

(*From somewhere far away, but very clear, come the voices of FREDA and JILL exactly as they spoke at the end of the little scene in the hall.*)

FREDA: (*Off.*) Why – mother – you look different.

JILL: (*Off.*) I know, darling – and I feel different. You see, I know. I suddenly saw – quite clearly – everything's all right – really all right – *now*…

THE FIGURE: You understand? She knows already.

JOHNSON: Can she read my mind?

THE FIGURE: Perhaps she reads a little further than your mind.

JOHNSON: You can pull back that hood now and show your face, my friend who calls me fool.

(*The FIGURE pulls back the hood, the golden shaft of light grows stronger, and now instead of an indeterminate face there is the face of a handsome young man, like an Apollo.*)

THE FIGURE: Yes, both are true. I have called you a fool, and I am your friend. And now you have a debt to discharge here.

JOHNSON: You said it would cost me nothing.

THE FIGURE: I said no money was necessary.

JOHNSON: Then how can I pay you?

THE FIGURE: (*Gravely.*) With thanks. And then it is
goodbye, Robert.

(*All the people in the CROWD, now in deep shadow, begin
to drift away, and as they go we just catch their low confused
voices saying: 'Goodbye Robert' and 'Goodbye Johnson' and
'Goodbye, Goodbye'. And then JOHNSON is left a solitary
figure in this steely shaft of light, while the FIGURE, shining
and golden, waits above on the stairs.*)

JOHNSON: (*With deep emotion.*) I have been a foolish,
greedy and ignorant man;

Yet I have had my time beneath the sun and stars;

I have known the returning strength and sweetness of the
seasons,

Blossom on the branch and the ripening of fruit,

The deep rest of the grass, the salt of the sea,

The frozen ecstasy of mountains.

The earth is nobler than the world we have built upon it;

The earth is long-suffering, solid, fruitful;

The world still shifting, dark, half-evil.

But what have I done that I should have a better world,

Even though there is in me something that will not rest

Until it sees Paradise…?

(*With very great emotion.*)

Farewell, all good things!

You will not remember me,

But I shall remember you…

THE FIGURE: (*Gravely.*) Robert Johnson, it is time now.

(*And here is the PORTER, standing just behind JOHNSON
with his hat and overcoat and bag.*)

PORTER: Your things, sir. (*Helps him on with his coat.*)

JOHNSON: (*Now with his overcoat on, holding his hat and bag,
with an echo of childish accents.*) For Thine is the kingdom,
the power and the glory…and God bless Jill and Freda
and Richard…and all my friends – and – and –
everybody…for ever and ever…Amen…

(*He puts on his hat and is now ready to go. He looks up at the
FIGURE, doubtfully.*)

(*Hesitantly.*) Is it – a long way?

THE FIGURE: (*Suddenly smiling like an angel.*) I don't
  know, Robert.
JOHNSON: (*Awkwardly.*) No...well...goodbye...

*A majestic theme has been announced, first only by the
woodwind. As JOHNSON still stands there, hesitating, the
light on the FIGURE fades, and then the whole staircase
disappears, leaving JOHNSON alone. He looks very small,
forlorn, for now the whole stage has been opened up to its
maximum size, and there is nothing there but JOHNSON.
The music marches on, with more and more instruments coming
in. JOHNSON looks about him, shivering a little, and turning
up the collar of his coat. And now there is a rapidly growing
intense blue light. The high curtains have gone at the back,
where it is bluer and bluer; until at last we see the glitter of
stars in space, and against them the curve of the world's rim.
As the brass blares out triumphantly and the drums roll and
the cymbals clash, JOHNSON, wearing his bowler hat and
carrying his bag, slowly turns and walks towards that blue
space and the shining constellations, and the curtain comes
down and the play is done.*